On the Wings of the Morning

RAF Bottesford 1941–1945

Vincent Holyoak

First published in 1995 by Vincent Holyoak
38 Wilberforce Road
Leicester
LE3 0GT

Typeset in Palatino. Made and printed in Great Britain by The Local History Press, 3 Devonshire Promenade, Lenton, Nottingham NG7 2DS.

ISBN 0 9526739 0 8

Front cover: On the 16th June 1942 photographer Charles E. Brown captured a formation of three 207 Squadron Lancasters over Cranwell. Closest to the camera is R5570 'F–Freddie', flown by F/Sgt Duxbury, which failed to return from Turin in December. Beyond is F/Sgt Nixon's L7583 'A–Apple' which survived the war, only to be scrapped. (RAF Museum)

Back cover: Sgt I.G. Boulton, flight engineer on F/O Doug Harvey RAAF's crew, 467 Squadron RAAF, gives the thumbs up, Bottesford late 1943. (C. Davies)

Contents

Preface

To the best of my knowledge, this is the first time that the war-time story of Bottesford has been told in full, probably because of the airfield's unique geographical location, falling as it does not neatly within one county, but across three. It was this neglect in comparison to other airfields that prompted me to attempt to remedy the situation, and I hope that what follows will be as much a revelation to the reader as it has been to me.

The title is inspired by the extract from Psalm 139 reproduced on one of the stained glass panels at the Royal Air Forces Memorial to the missing, Runnymede. I feel the choice is particularly apt when one considers that of the 346 aircrew killed while flying from Bottesford in the last war, 118 have no known grave. I make no excuses for having attempted to approach the story from a human angle rather than to aim for a dry repetition of official records, hence the reliance on extracts from interviews. I have tried through the extracts to convey something of the individual suffering, sacrifices, but above all, of the pride and the self deprecating humour of the veterans interviewed. In conclusion, this is very much their story, and I have been privileged to have been given the opportunity to tell it.

Vincent Holyoak
Leicester
September 1995

Acknowledgements

By far the hardest task has been deciding what to leave out, and for those people who were so generous with their time but do not see their contributions reproduced here, I hope they will forgive me. Literally hundreds of people have helped me over the years in various ways and, although it would be wrong to single out individuals, that is what I will begin by doing! I would like to offer particular thanks to my parents and Michelle for their encouragement throughout, and to Bill Baguley and Frank Slack for all their help, advice — and above all — their friendship. Thanks also to Ted Richardson of the 467/463 Association, Cynthia Brown for the difficult and time consuming task of editing, and to Susan Howard for her hard work in preparing the manuscript for publication. Also to Denise Rope for permission to use quotations from the diary of George Hawes, first printed in her book *For the Duration*. It goes without saying that any errors, ommissions or inaccuracies are solely my own. I should also like to acknowledge the generous help of the following organizations and periodicals over the years:
Aircrew Association, Bomber Command Association, Royal Air Force Association, *Leicester Mercury*, *Brighton Evening Argus*, *Southampton Evening Echo*, Tavistock Newspapers Limited, *FlyPast* Magazine, *After the Battle* Magazine, Airfield Research Group, Humberside Libraries, Devon C.R.O., Humberside C.R.O., Lincolnshire C.R.O., Commonwealth War Graves Commission, Public Records Office Kew, Air Historical Branch of the Ministry of Defence, RAF Museum Hendon, Department of Air Force History Washington D.C., Australian War Memorial Canberra, 207 Squadron Association, 467/463 Squadron Association, 77 Squadron Association, 90 Squadron Association, 50th Troop Carrier Wing Association.

Thanks also to:
C.Allen, N.Atkin, M.Baggaley, J.K.Banfield, D.Barnes,P.G.Barry, K.Batchelor, A.W.Bates, K.H.P.Beauchamp, L.Beauchamp, F.J.Belfitt, D.Bentley, H.C.J.Bentley, J.Berridge, S.Bethell, S.Bray, M.Butterworth, A.Cackett, C.A.Campbell, A.Camps, J.W.Carr, M.I.Claridge, W.S.Close, J.Collier, G.D.Currie, C.Davies, A.D.Dick, T.E.Done, A.R.C.Donohue, E.Dring, C.B.Edwards, F.Ehrman, F.Fazackerley, K.Ferris, D.V.Forbes, G.E.Fitt, J.George, R.Glynne-Owen, W.H.Goldstraw, B.Goodwin, D.A.Green, P.H.T.Green, P.Greenwood, A.Hallam, B.R.W.Hallows, W.J.Hamilton, G.C.Harrison, R.Hare, D.A.Harriman, H.M.Hart, C.Hawes, H.Hernaman, R.Holland, R.Holyoak, M.Honeybone, S.Hooper, D.Ikin, V.Johnson, A.Jordan, M.Kaye, R.Kirby, M.C.Lillie, I.McInnes, W.Manifold, B.M.Mason, N.Meglio, D.Moore, J.Nedwich, M.Palmer, A.Parsons, S.E.Pattinson, J.Paxton, R.Pearson, J.Pickford, E.Povey, P.M.Rae, G.Rawley, M.A.Riddell, J.E.Rimmington, D.J.Roper, F.A.Roper, J.Rose, N.Rushton, J. van Puyenbroek, J.Scott, R.Shaw, C.Smith, P.Sortehaug, C.Spedding, E.B.Spooner, R.Stamford, C.F.Steer, R.Storey, N.Suddery, D.Sullivan, D.S.Symonds, K.F.Thiele, M.L.Thornes, A.Tongue, G.Tothill, F.Townsend, J.B.Walker, M.Walker, P.Ward-Hunt, H.Watson, W.Weinkam, M.Wells, E.Whatley, R.Williamson, M.Wolfe, G.Woodhouse, K.L.Worden, A.T.Youdan.

CHAPTER ONE

Don't you know there's a war on?

Zeppelin! — the very name was enough to strike terror into the hearts of British civilians during the First World War. In reality the German airships did little damage and inflicted only minor casualties, but they clearly showed the psychological effect of air attacks on the morale of the civil population. As usual, popular hysteria was fanned by the press who made much of the fact that Britain's island status could no longer guarantee protection from attack. The attacks had also fired the imagination of military theorists who predicted that air power would play a decisive role in any future conflict, a belief which they clung onto when there were attempts to disband the RAF in the 1920s. From 1934 onwards the service began a programme of expansion to counter the threat posed by Nazi Germany. Although by 1937 it had doubled in size, at the outbreak of war in 1939 the Air Ministry knew that a further expansion in aircraft, aircrew training and aerodromes was needed. By the summer of 1940 the defeat in France had shown beyond any doubt that Britain's only remaining means of offensive action was by air power — chiefly the bomber. Within a few months the largest scheme of public works ever seen in Britain — one which would change the face of the English landscape irrevocably — was beginning. A workforce of 60,000 men was rapidly engaged in airfield construction. By December 1944 the number of available airfields had expanded from a pre-war total of 170 to 670 and at the peak of construction in 1942 one new airfield was opening every three days at a cost of around £1,000,000 each (roughly equivalent to £18,000,000 in 1995). Like all counties, Leicestershire and Nottinghamshire were not excluded. In 1939 they had a combined total of just six airfields[1], but by 1945 this had risen to 28. Lincolnshire, in comparison, because of its proximity to Germany, had 45 operational aerodromes, more than any other county.

The task of supplying new airfields was the responsibility of the Air Ministry's Directorate-General of Works who scanned maps for promising sites, then despatched engineers to examine them first-hand. They looked for possible obstructions in the vicinity, examined the soil and made their recommendations. It was on such an errand that 'the men from the Ministry' arrived in the quiet rural parish of Bottesford in Leicestershire.

Situated in the beautiful Vale of Belvoir, Bottesford is mostly known for its 13th century parish church, St. Mary's whose spire, the tallest in the county, is visible for miles. The church was built under the patronage of the Earls of

[1] Desford (1935), Braunstone (1935), Rearsby (1938), Hucknall (1915), Tollerton (1930) and Newton (1937).

Rutland whose family seat, Belvoir Castle, looks down on the Vale from a nearby ridge. Like all villages in the Vale, for centuries Bottesford owed its living to corn. Such was the prosperity of the Duke's estates that even the industrial revolution and the growth of nearby large manufacturing cities such as Nottingham and Leicester had little effect. Despite the construction of a canal in the 1790s and a railway sixty years later, change was slow to come, and was resisted by successive Dukes as much as possible. But times were indeed changing and in 1920 much of the estate had to be sold off to pay death duties. A few tenants were finally able to buy the farms tended by their families for generations, although others were unable to raise the money and became homeless. It was on some of these 'lucky' former tenants that the Air Ministry invoked the full force of the Emergency Powers (Defence) Act 1939 and gave them just a few days to pack their belongings and leave their land.

The Air Ministry's surveyors had found two suitable sites in the Vale. The first was close to the village of Langar in Nottinghamshire; the second covered an area of 700 acres north of Bottesford around the hamlet of Normanton, where the counties of Leicestershire, Nottinghamshire and Lincolnshire meet. RAF policy was to operate aerodromes in groups of two or three, with a 'parent' station administering one or two 'satellites', so the site at Normanton was chosen as the parent and Langar as the satellite. After the requisition orders had been served various tenders were considered and the contracts for both Normanton and Langar were awarded to George Wimpey and Co. Like several other well-known builders, Wimpeys were to make their fortune in the wartime airfield construction programme. They began work at Normanton in the winter of 1940/41 under the direction of the No.17 Works Area Superintendent Engineer, Mr Thompson. Their first task was to build a prefabricated hangar on the edge of the hamlet into which convoys of lorries began unloading materials, most of which arrived via the LNER railway and Bottesford station. Alongside the hangar Wimpeys built a canteen for their workmen staffed by local women. A few building workers lived on site, but the majority, mostly Irishmen, were ferried daily from Nottingham in buses chartered from the South Notts. Bus Company. In the first few weeks over twelve miles of hedgerows were torn out, the site levelled, and drainage pipes connected with the Ease Drain, a field dyke running eastwards from Normanton. Throughout the war the heavy clay soil made waterlogging a constant problem. In wet weather the landing ground became a quagmire and the run-off from hangars and runways turned the Ease Drain into a raging torrent.

Once the site had been levelled the concrete perimeter track and runways followed. The aerodrome was built to the standard Class 'A' bomber configuration with three runways arranged in a triangle. The low power-to-weight ratios of aircraft in those days meant that to get airborne they had to take off into the wind in order to obtain maximum lift. The aerodrome's main runway, built parallel to the Normanton-Bennington road was 1900 yards long, 50 yards in width and aligned to the prevailing wind. If the wind

RAF Bottesford
Left: general location.
Below: layout of airfield as of 1945.

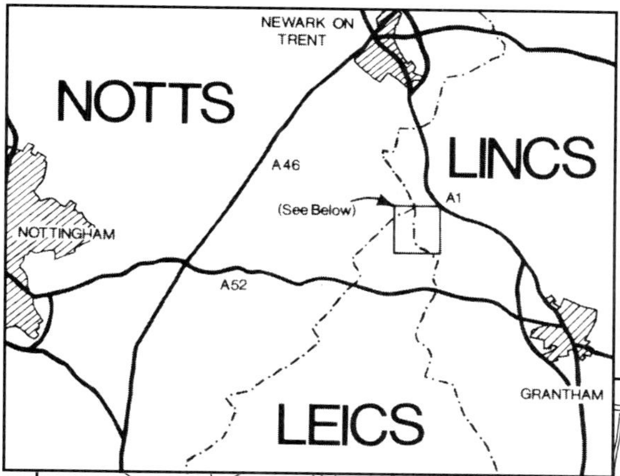

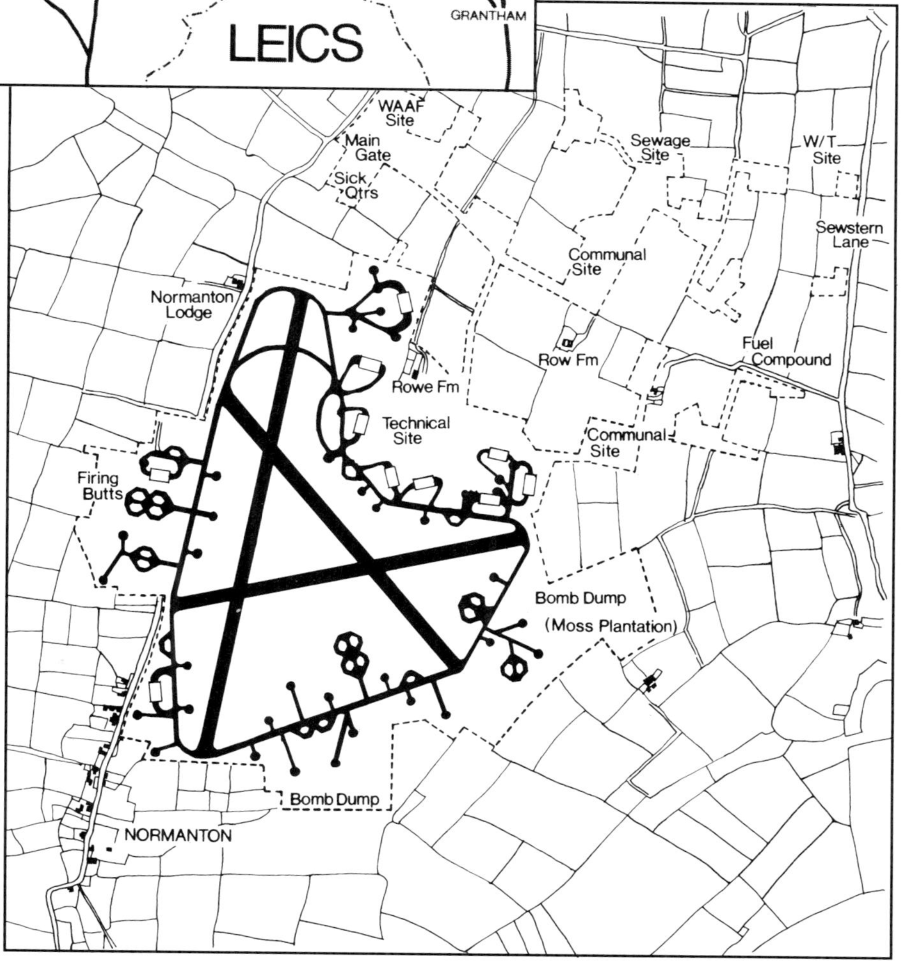

changed, takeoffs could be switched to either of the two subsidiary runways. At the same time three further T2 hangars were constructed on the technical site around Rowe Farm and a start was made on the hundreds of prefabricated buildings, equivalent to a small town, which were needed to run the aerodrome and house its staff. In order to reduce the threat of air attack the sleeping huts, mess halls and station sick quarters were spread out across fifteen separate sites to the north. Miles of concrete roads and power lines had to be laid connecting them. A High Frequency transmitting station was placed opposite Beck Farm by an ancient droveway known as Sewstern Lane and a Direction Finding Station was placed in a meadow south of Normanton Thorns where the three counties actually meet. This meant that although the main gate and the SSQ were in Nottinghamshire, the guard hut a few feet behind, the technical site and living sites were all in Lincolnshire. To further confuse matters the main runway and the bomb dump were squarely in Leicestershire!

After almost a year of work RAF Station Bottesford officially opened on September 10th 1941 in No.5 (Bomber) Group under the command of Group Captain W.G. Cheshire[1]. Although closer to Normanton than Bottesford, whenever possible it was Air Ministry policy to name aerodromes after the parish in which they were built. Nonetheless, several of the sites remained unfinished, and when five days after the station had opened the Air Officer Commanding 5 Group, Air Vice-Marshal John Slessor made known his wishes to have the aerodrome operational within one month, the Ministry of Works redoubled their efforts to hurry Wimpeys along. They were unsuccessful, and when Group Captain Cheshire inspected the building work at the start of November, he described progress 'far from satisfactory'. Although part of the delay was due to the decision to extend the main runway, at Langar the problems were even greater, for here the main runway had been built on the wrong axis and had to be completely torn up and started again!

Nevertheless, on September 22nd a Wellington bomber tested Bottesford's runways for the first time, and soon afterwards permission was granted for 12 Secondary Flying Training School at Grantham to use them for practice circuits and landings. The first of their aircraft, a Proctor piloted by Wing Commander Corbley, dropped in briefly on October 11th. Four days later the airfield's 'Drem lighting' — essential for night flying — was tested for the first time.

At dusk on a chilly night soon afterwards the airfield's beacon was hitched on to a three ton truck, towed to position down a nearby lane and switched on, flashing out the station's coded identity letters 'AQ' in morse for the first time. Bottesford was finally ready for action. Over the next two years the beacon took on a special significance for the tired bomber crews circling above in the darkness waiting their turn to land, because it meant they had made it. They were home, they were safe, and for a few short hours at least they could sleep and try to forget the horrors of the night.

[1] Later Air Chief Marshal Sir Walter Cheshire, Air Aide-de-camp to HM the Queen.

CHAPTER TWO

'Leicester's Own'

Since late September 1941 the Avro Manchester bombers of 207 Squadron had become frequent visitors to the aerodrome. Squadron Leader Beauchamp had been first to test the runways in an unladen aircraft, and was followed a few days later by the C.O., Wing Commander Lewis in a Manchester loaded up to the maximum all-up weight, 45,000 lbs. These activities were explained by Group Captain Cheshire's visit to RAF Waddington to discuss arrangements for 207's impending move to Bottesford. It was a particularly apt choice for Leicestershire's only front-line aerodrome of the last war. In the immediate pre-war period the RAF had mounted a campaign to increase public support by encouraging cities to adopt squadrons officially, and in June 1939 the *Leicester Mercury* reported:

Leicester was not mentioned when the scheme for the affiliation of RAF squadrons to principal cities and town of the country was announced in April last, but the Air Ministry announces new affiliations including that of 207 Bomber Squadron to Leicester. The Squadron will pay an annual ceremonial visit to Leicester, and it is understood, will give a display at Leicester Air Port. On this occasion the public will be afforded an opportunity of inspecting aircraft when on the ground and meeting the crews. The Squadron, which will 'watch over Leicester', will probably co-operate with other air interests in important civic events, providing Service commitments permit. The total number of towns now affiliated to RAF Squadrons is 59. Several members of No.207 Squadron are Leicester-born men.

Although the outbreak of war meant that the ties between the city and the Squadron were never formally cemented, the story came full-circle in 1989 when the Squadron's Roll of Honour was placed next to its standard in Leicester Cathedral. As the *Mercury* remarked, many of 207's men had local connections, not just with Leicester, but with the East Midlands generally. Flight Sergeant Roger Rowlands, an air gunner, came from Scraptoft near Leicester and was the grandson of a Bottesford horse breeder. From Nottingham came Sergeant Jack Culley, a former insurance salesman from Netherfield, and Sergeants Eric Cartwright and Claude Westbury; and from Sherwood, Sergeant George Duke. All four were killed flying from Bottesford in 1942. Amongst the groundcrews were Nottingham born armourers Arthur Giles, George Thompson, Ernie Spooner and Dennis Bentley. Throughout the war the Midlands' industrial cities provided a rich source of recruits for the technical trades.

207 Squadron itself had a history dating back to 1916, and after various incarnations had been reformed at Waddington in November 1940 to introduce to service the first of the RAF's new generation of heavy bombers, the Avro Manchester. In many respects the Manchester was an innovative design. With a bomb bay 33 feet in length it could accommodate a warload of 5 tons, greater than any other bomber then in RAF service, but because it was such an improvement on many other types Bomber Command was forced to fly, it had been rushed into service long before it was ready. Aside from problems with stability, finally solved by fitting a larger tail section, there were two other concerns. First and foremost were the engines, its Rolls-Royce Vultures. Six years in development, the Vulture was a novel design attempting to mate together two 12-cylinder 'vee' engine blocks around a single crankshaft to produce an 'x' configured 24-cylinder engine, theoretically with the power of two normal units. It was hoped that this would save weight, but unfortunately the Vulture produced far less power than expected, and problems with oil circulation made seizures and engine fires common. To make matters worse, underpowered as it was, the aircraft would not stay airborne for long on one engine! The other problem was the elaborate hydraulic system which powered the gun turrets, the undercarriage, bomb doors and flaps. Leaks and pressure failures were commonplace but, as with the engines, Bomber Command was in such a desperate situation that it could not afford to withdraw the aircraft to rectify the faults. For this reason, by the time that the Manchester was entering service it had already been decided that it would be replaced as soon as possible by an uprated four-engined model using the tried and tested Rolls-Royce Merlins. Although referred to for security reasons as the Manchester III, this improved model eventually became known as the Lancaster. In the meantime, against all the odds 207 did much to overcome chronic serviceability problems. Even so, Flying Officer John de Lacy Wooldridge (or 'Dim' as he was better known) summed up the general feeling on the Squadron by carrying his greatcoat on operations, saying in explanation 'I'm damned if I'll be cold in a prisoner of war camp!'.

At 10 am on November 15th 1941 207 Squadron's fifteen serviceable Manchesters took off from Waddington, overflew the station in salute, and made for Bottesford where they landed a few minutes afterwards. The lorries carrying the Squadron's personnel did not begin arriving until dusk when some attempt was made to assign billets. Dennis Bentley, then a 19-year-old armourer remembered the misery of splashing through the mud in his 'best blues'. Having been paraded in the rain earlier that morning he and his companions only leant of their destination when the driver of their lorry stopped to ask directions, all the signposts having been removed to hinder German paratroopers. The confusion didn't improve on arrival. Everywhere in the darkness men were shouting, cursing and swearing as they stumbled along with heavy kitbags. When Dennis finally reached his hut on a sleeping site off Sewstern Lane, it was to discover that there were no straw palliasses and only two sodden blankets each. Worse still, there was nothing to light

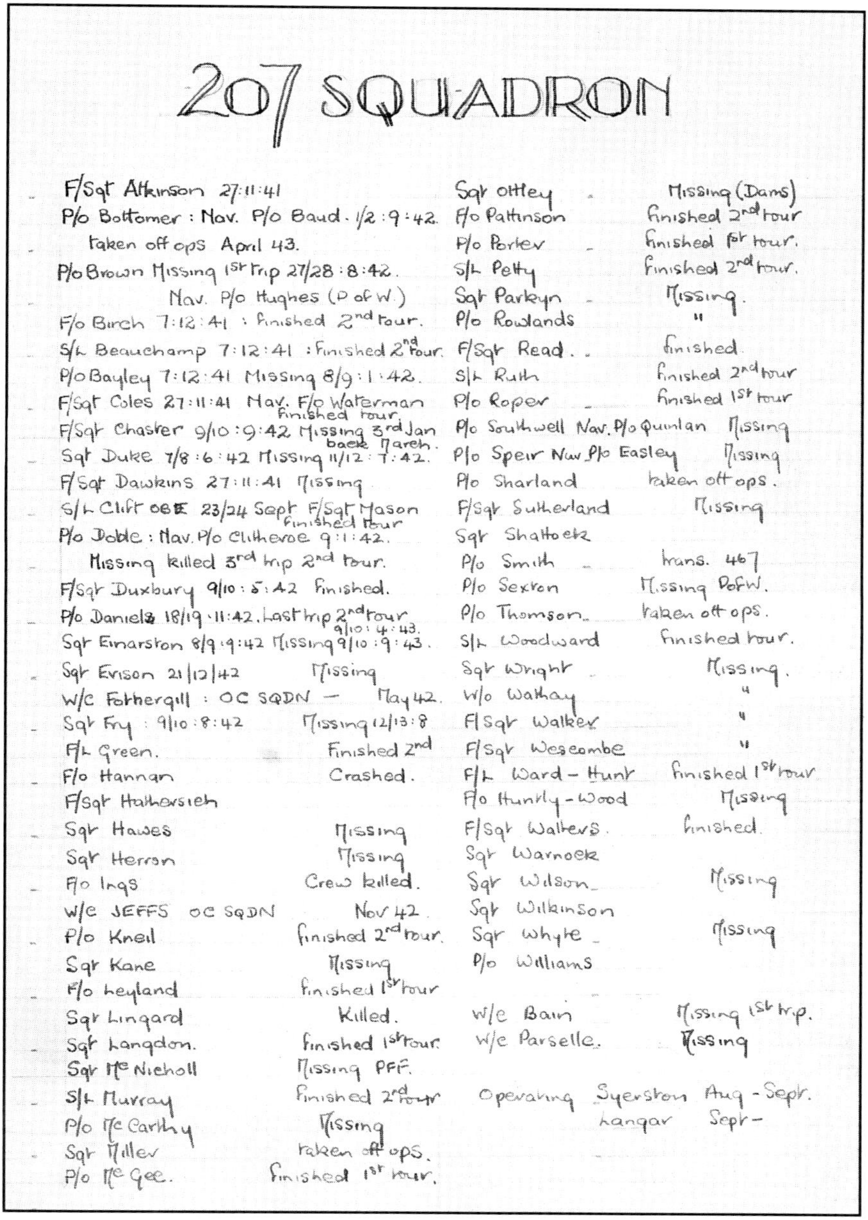

207 SQUADRON

F/Sgt Atkinson 27:11:41		Sgt Ottley	Missing (Dams)
P/O Bottomer : Nav. P/O Baud. 1/2:9:42.		F/O Pattinson	finished 2nd tour
taken off ops April 43.		P/O Porter	finished 1st tour.
P/O Brown Missing 1st trip 27/28:8:42.		S/L Petty	Finished 2nd tour.
Nav. P/O Hughes (P of W.)		Sgt Parkyn	Missing.
F/O Birch 7:12:41 : finished 2nd tour.		P/O Rowlands	"
S/L Beauchamp 7:12:41 : Finished 2nd tour.		F/Sgt Read	finished
P/O Bayley 7:12:41 Missing 8/9:1:42.		S/L Ruth	finished 2nd tour
F/Sgt Coles 27:11:41 Nav. F/O Waterman finished tour.		P/O Roper	finished 1st tour
F/Sgt Chaster 9/10:9:42 Missing 3rd Jan back March.		P/O Southwell Nav. P/O Quinlan	Missing
Sgt Duke 7/8:6:42 Missing 11/12:7:42.		P/O Speir Nav P/O Easley	Missing
F/Sgt Dawkins 27:11:41 Missing		P/O Sharland	taken off ops.
S/L Clift OBE 23/24 Sept F/Sgt Mason finished tour		F/Sgt Sutherland	Missing
P/O Doble : Nav. P/O Clitheroe 9:1:42.		Sgt Shattock	
Missing killed 3rd trip 2nd tour.		P/O Smith	trans. 467
F/Sgt Duxbury 9/10:5:42 finished.		P/O Sexton	Missing PofW.
P/O Daniels 18/19:11:42. Last trip 2nd tour 9/10:4:43.		P/O Thomson	taken off ops.
Sgt Einarston 8/9:9:42 Missing 9/10:9:43.		S/L Woodward	finished tour.
Sgt Evison 21/12/42	Missing	Sgt Wright	Missing.
W/C Fothergill : OC SQDN —	May 42.	W/O Wathey	"
Sgt Fry : 9/10:8:42	Missing 12/13:8	F/Sgt Walker	"
F/L Green.	Finished 2nd	F/Sgt Wescombe	"
F/O Hannan	Crashed.	F/L Ward-Hunt	finished 1st tour
F/Sgt Hathersich		F/O Huntly-Wood	Missing
Sgt Hawes	Missing	F/Sgt Walters.	finished.
Sgt Herron	Missing	Sgt Warnock	
F/O Ings	Crew killed.	Sgt Wilson	Missing
W/C JEFFS OC SQDN	Nov 42.	Sgt Wilkinson	
P/O Kneil	finished 2nd tour.	Sgt Whyte	Missing
Sgt Kane	Missing	P/O Williams	
F/O Leyland	finished 1st tour		
Sgt Lingard	Killed.	W/C Bain	Missing 1st trip.
Sgt Langdon.	finished 1st tour.	W/C Parselle.	Missing
Sgt McNicholl	Missing PFF.		
S/L Murray	Finished 2nd tour	Operating Syerston Aug - Sept.	
P/O McCarthy	Missing	Langar Sept -	
Sgt Miller	taken off ops.		
P/O McGee.	finished 1st tour.		

A page reproduced from the scrapbook of S/O Marie Cooper, a WAAF Intelligence Officer at Bottesford, showing the fates of crew captains on 207 Squadron. (M.Claridge)

207 Squdron Armourers amid the appalling conditions at Bottesford during the winter of 1941–2. Left to right: Smithers, F/Sgt Weatherall, Eric, Bob Waldrer, Dennis Bentley, Bill Freeman, Ron Walker, 'Ginge', 'Housie', Alf, George, Eric King, Alan and Vic. (D. Bentley)

the coke stove. Sergeant Frank Belfitt, observer on Jimmy Kneil's crew, had flown in earlier that same day and was equally unimpressed.

Waddington was a 1936 purpose-built station, comfortable and convenient to Lincoln for our forays on our nights off. No such luck with Bottesford! Our first impression was of a sea of mud, and one stepped off the concrete pathways at one's peril. It was damp and miserable when we landed there, and it stayed that way! It seemed as though it were built on one vast bog. Bottesford was not a station one was happy about — mud and more mud: isolated and forlorn. My mother used to send me honey and Ryvita to keep me going. She imagined I was at the North Pole or somewhere — she wasn't far wrong!

Sergeant 'Goldie' Goldstraw, observer on Flying Officer Dave Green's crew also had vivid memories of that first winter:

When we arrived the workmen were still finishing off many of the construction tasks, and there was liquid mud all over the place. Sleeping accommodation was very poor; the wooden huts were cold and draughty and let the rain in. The room which I shared with the rear gunner was often awash. The concrete base on which the solid fuel stove was perched was always full of water, and it would have been impossible to light a fire even if we could have obtained coal. Bedding, clothing and personal effects were always damp, so we slept in trousers and shirts under the blankets. Most of the time was spent in the Sergeants' Mess on the communal site where at least we could be warm and dry.

So bleak were the surroundings that according to the diary of an Australian pilot, Flight Sergeant George Hawes, Canadian members of the Squadron half expected Indians to come whooping over the hill! The biggest shock after the compact Waddington was the distance between sites, and although this was eased by the issue of bicycles, sticks had to be carried to clean off the mud which clogged wheels and prevented them turning. Mud was not a problem confined to bicycles, for over the first weeks several aircraft became bogged when pilots accidentally put wheels off taxi tracks or dispersals. Each aircraft weighed something over thirteen tons unloaded, and it was no mean feat to free them once caught.

Since wing Commander Lewis had tested Bottesford's runways some weeks before, command of 207 had passed to Wing Commander Charles Fothergill. Always dapper and sporting a luxuriant moustache, he rarely flew and delegated this responsibility to his two flight commanders. In charge of 'A' Flight was Squadron Leader 'Thos' Murray who had joined the Squadron back in April 1941. Prior to that he had flown an extended tour of operations on 49 Squadron which was where he first met Squadron Leader K.H.P. Beauchamp, now commanding 207's 'B' Flight. In appearance the tall angular 'Beach' contrasted sharply with 'Thos' Murray, whose balding head made him appear far older than his years. In fact both men were aged just 25. Coinciding with 207's move was the appointment of Group Captain F.R.D. Swain as station commander. A career officer, in 1936 'Ferdie' Swain had won the world altitude record for Britain by taking a Bristol 138A up to 49,967 feet, for which he had been awarded the AFC. On a later transatlantic trip he met the American lady who was to become his wife, and often boasted in the Mess that on the return he had been allowed to take the controls of the Dornier X flying boat, the flagship of Nazism.

Six days after 207's arrival two crews were rostered to take part in the very first operation from the aerodrome. Piloting L7319 'EM-X', one of the Squadron's oldest aircraft, was Flight Lieutenant W.D.B. Ruth DFC, whilst flying L7432 'EM-J' was Flight Sergeant B.C. Wescombe. The latter was considered 207's 'lucky' Manchester as it had been nursed back from Berlin on one engine the previous August to earn its pilot a DSO. The story was that it would have been a VC, but this was considered too much of an adverse comment on the Manchester's unreliability! Twenty-four year-old 'Babe' Ruth and 25-year-old Basil Wescombe had both just begun their second tours, but because it was then customary to fly a complete tour as second pilot before becoming a captain on 'heavies' they were still considered 'freshmen'. Their mission was to attack German submarines in the French port of Lorient, and theirs would be the only Manchesters taking part, the rest of the force comprising 51 Hampdens, all from 5 Group.

At this point in the war Bomber Command was expending an increasing amount of effort in attacking enemy ports. German U-Boats operating in the

First of the many. F/Lt W.D.B. Ruth DFC and F/Sgt B.C. Wescombe carried out the first raid of the war from Bottesford on the night of 23/24th November 1941: neither survived the war. (M. Claridge/A.R.C. Donohue)

Atlantic were enjoying increasing success in their efforts to cut off Britain's ship-borne supply lifeline, added to which the capital ships *Scharnhorst*, *Gneisenau* and *Prinz Eugen*, sheltering under heavy protection in Brest harbour were threatening at any moment to break out into the Atlantic and cause further havoc with the merchant convoys. Since the Royal Navy was already hopelessly overstretched, the obvious solution was to ask the RAF to attack any ports where there were signs of enemy naval activity.

Secondly, and perhaps most critical of all, in August 1941 the Government-sponsored Butt report had concluded that RAF bombing attacks had been depressingly ineffective, with only a fifth of crews managing to get within five miles of the target. Appalling losses at the outbreak of the war has shown that Bomber Command's aircraft could not defend themselves in daylight, so the switch had been made to night attacks. But the crews had little experience in navigation at night, and with the unsuitable equipment available, even in good weather, whole cities, let alone specific targets were proving impossible to hit. This would soon lead to the controversial decision to use 'area bombing'[1]. But in the meantime, not only were German

[1] A directive was issued on February 14th 1942 which stipulated that in future whole cities rather than just the industrial targets within them were to be attacked.

targets still defying air attacks, they were also inflicting escalating casualties on the raiders, the average life of a heavy bomber being just fourteen sorties. After a disastrous raid on Berlin on November 7/8th 1941, Bomber Command was ordered to curtail its attacks on inland German targets, with the result that ports would receive most of its attention for some time to come.

Sunday 23rd November 1941 saw the beginning of the daily routine that was to continue at Bottesford for the next two years. Groundcrews were split into two flights, 'A' and 'B', and every morning would make their way to the aircraft dotted on their dispersals around the aerodrome. First job was the daily inspections which included routine checks of airframe, hydraulics, engines and coolant levels, and then the engines were run up one by one to check 'magneto drop'. Meanwhile, instrument 'bashers' and wireless technicians would be carrying out their own tests whilst the armourers cleaned and installed the Browning .303 machine guns in each turret. Cold and icy as they were, the aircraft were not easy to work on. For those working in the biting winds which swept the flights in winter there were two alternatives; either wrap up well and sacrifice mobility, or simply freeze to death! The various combinations of clothing reflected their occupants' trades and personal preferences, and although gloves were impractical, given the mud which coated everyone and everything, gumboots were a necessity.

Having checked their names on the roster in the Flight Office, the aircrews appeared mid-morning to give their allotted aircraft a 'Night Flying Test'. Assuming nothing was amiss, after taxiing back to the dispersal the captain would sign the Form 700 to say that he accepted the aircraft as serviceable. The crews then cycled back up the hill to wile away the hours before briefing as best they could, reading newspapers in the Mess, listening to gramophone records in their huts, catching up with correspondence or perhaps pensively smoking a cigarette. In 1941 briefings were still relatively informal affairs held in the 'Ops' Block behind Station Headquarters. The red tape pinned to the wall map gave them their route, the Met. Officer told them the weather situation and the Intelligence Officer would describe the target and its importance. Individual timings, attack heights, bomb settings and other details were left to the captains and their observers. Then finally, after briefing, it was another cycle ride to the messes for the pre-flight meal.

Meanwhile the fuel and oil tanks on the Manchesters were being topped up and the warloads prepared. Tonight each would be carrying ten 500 lb General Purpose bombs. Since October daily convoys from Norton Disney had stocked the bomb dump to capacity. The bombs were taken from storage to the fusing hut, and from there out to the aircraft on long trolleys. Small winches were then manhandled into the aircraft, their cables pushed through holes in the roof of the bomb bay, and the bombs, already on shackles, generally pushed, pulled and sweated into place. Then it was only a matter of connecting the electrical leads in the bay and checking the circuits so that the shackles disengaged when the bomb aimer pressed the 'tit'. Such mundane activities were common to all bomber airfields, but as the groundcrews busied themselves on Wescombe and Ruth's aircraft that afternoon, something decidedly out of the ordinary was unfolding just a few miles away. Pilot Officer Bill Hills had been asked to fly two groundstaff and two fellow pilots to Waddington in Manchester L7300 'EM-F'. He had hoped to use the opportunity for a spot of low-level flying, but as his 21-year-old wireless operator, Sergeant Charles Smith from Beverley recalled:

After being airborne for only a few minutes one of the engines failed, but having decided we could still get to Waddington we informed them of our approach and carried on hopefully. Unfortunately on the other side of Lincoln the other engine faltered and we made a rapid descent. The skipper managed to keep control until when coming down over a railway embankment the rear turret broke off and we slithered down the other side into a lake which had once been a gravel quarry. We all managed to get out of the rapidly sinking fuselage with the aid of the air sea rescue rubber dinghy and a severely shocked angler who had been fishing from a punt. This was listing badly itself, having been flooded by our crashing aircraft! There were no fatalities but a few broken limbs and other injuries. We revived ourselves by drinking the bottles of rum from the first aid equipment, and this helped keep out the cold, as we were soaking wet, and being November it was bitterly cold.

Sergeant John van Puyenbroek, the other Wireless Operator/Air Gunner on Bill Hills' crew also has cause to remember that afternoon:

The second pilot, Pilot Officer Plaistowe, was standing up when we crashed and hit his head on the instrument panel sustaining concussion and a suspected fractured skull in the process. On the bank near the lake was 'Applegarth' cottage and the occupants stripped Plaistowe off, dried him and wrapped him in a rug, leaving him dressed only in a pair of dripping wet socks. The ambulance had been called but after nearly an hour had not appeared, and the fisherman with us said he would drive us to Lincoln hospital. We set off and as we turned by Lincoln's Stonebow into the High Street, Plaistowe yanked at the door handle and was off down the street — naked — leaving his rug by the car. It was now late afternoon and being Sunday there were countless airmen walking their girlfriends along the 'monkey-run'. Plaistowe's eyes were staring wildly, he was showing all the signs of concussion, and the girls began to scream. After a few yards he was brought to a halt by a large Lincolnshire bobbie. Almost at the same time an ambulance came tearing down the High Street, bell ringing, realised we were probably from the crash and stopped...

*We were put straight to bed, unwashed, stinking, wounds drying up by now; the big cups of tea the nurses brought in tasted marvellous. The next morning, Plaistowe started doing handstands on the end of his bed until the nurses saw him and tucked him in again! As a sequel to the crash, when the Maintenance Unit boys started the salvage operation a civilian approached them and said 'We want this ****ing wreck out of here by next Saturday — we've got a fishing competition on!' Life could be difficult for some civilians at that time...!'*

The wreck of Manchester L7300 'F–Freddie', in Fiskerton Quarry lake after P/O Bill Hills' miraculous crash-landing. (P.H.T. Green)

Back at Bottesford, Ruth took off at two minutes to five into the darkness, Wescombe following minutes later. After the drama that afternoon, the raid itself was uneventful:

Flight Lieutenant Ruth (DFC) described his trip as the most enjoyable he had ever had. Conditions, he said, were those of a summer night. Visibility over the whole route, both to the target and back to Coningsby (where he had been instructed to 'home') were excellent... The dock installations were easily picked out and bursts were observed from the bombs in the target area. No results, however, were seen...Flight Sergeant Wescombe made a similar trip enjoying equally good conditions...

CHAPTER THREE

Target for tonight

The waning moon at the end of November 1941 was accompanied by deteriorating weather across the whole of northern Europe. Whilst aircraft could take off in low cloud or fog, landing was another matter and, if there were no airfields to which they could be diverted, they were in trouble. Although each aerodrome had a Direction Finding station which could obtain a radio fix and provide a course to reach the runway, approaches in poor visibility were fraught with danger. Altimeters were only accurate to fifty feet, and if a pilot misjudged and let down too rapidly the result was often fatal. Equally, he might only see the ground at the last moment and not leave enough space to stop. If he was quick he could open out the throttles and go around again. Unfortunately the Manchester's Vultures often failed to respond to sudden bursts of throttle, leading to a loss of airspeed, height, and a collision with either the ground or any obstructions beyond the threshold. Bottesford was far from ideal for this. Three hundred yards north of the main runway were woods, the SSQ and WAAF sites. Half a mile in the opposite direction lay Beacon Hill, 199 feet above sea level, and beyond that the spire of St. Mary's church. To make matters worse, the Vale of Belvoir was particularly susceptible to fog, so until March when Bottesford was fitted with the new Standard Beam Approach radio aid for landings in poor visibility, bad weather meant a stand-down from 'ops'.

One evening during this same period, December 7th to be precise, Flying Officer Peter Ward-Hunt was listening to the wireless in the Mess when he heard some news which compelled him to wake his friend, 21-year-old Frank Roper. The item which caused so much excitement told of the Japanese attack on Pearl Harbor. Although greeted with horror and outrage in America, in Britain it gave rise to a new sense of optimism. She had been fighting alone since June 1940, and 1941 had been a particularly bleak year; but when, four days after Pearl Harbor Germany and Italy declared war on America, she had a formidable ally. The news held particular significance for Roper, because although a Pilot Officer in the RCAF, he was actually an American, born in Washington D.C. He had wanted more than anything to fly, but lacked the necessary qualifications to enlist in the Air Corps, so when in 1940 a friend joined the RCAF Roper did the same. Under U.S. law he faced a ten year jail sentence and a $20,000 fine for doing so, but he believed that America would enter the war eventually anyway — besides which, the recruiting officer told him that his American citizenship was not a problem, and that he could merely dispense with the usual pledge of allegiance to the King. Roper joined 207 at Waddington as second pilot on David Green's crew before being given his own crew when Green was posted 'tour-expired' in February 1942.

For the most part the last weeks of 1941 were spent practising formation flying and cross-countries. There was little enthusiasm when it was revealed that a lack of results against the ships in Brest meant that attacks were to be switched to daylight, an almost suicidal prospect in an underpowered and poorly armed heavy bomber. For 207 the point was rammed home two days before Christmas when two stragglers from a formation of six Manchesters were attacked by Spitfires in fading light over the North Sea. Only one aircraft, R5782 EM-R piloted by Flight Sergeant Geoff Dawkins, was damaged. It returned safely to Bottesford, the fighters having broken off when they saw the RAF markings, but it was a salutary lesson.

As the station came to life the trickle of women from the Women's Auxiliary Air Force gradually increased as they took over jobs done by airmen. All trades were open to women excepting armourer and aircrew, but the idea of women actually doing the jobs took far longer to accept. Among those arriving in December was Section Officer Marie Cooper, one of the first women trained in Intelligence duties. Capable and determined, well-read and well travelled as she was, life at Bottesford was a shock to her.

The WAAF quarters were not yet finished so I was billeted on a local farmer with a bicycle for transport. I broke the oil lamps regularly through inexpert use. There were hams and onions hanging from the ceiling of a vast kitchen, a strange dialect and a routine in the household largely unchanged from Elizabethan times, chamberpots and all! There were three generations in the farmhouse and the daughter was on the point of delivery of another child. This duly occurred with the ceremony of lying in state in a special bedroom to receive the congratulations from a stream of visitors on the following morning. It was an incredible time, and a sharp contrast to the Manchester aircraft flying above and at war!

Some villagers resented the war for the influx of outsiders that it had brought into their small community. They were not alone. A few older officers and NCOs objected to the presence of women on the station, particularly since they were temporarily forced to share messes with the men. Marie Cooper remembered that one ground staff officer wrote a piece in the Mess 'Line Book' (usually used for good-natured boasts and 'line-shoots') predicting what would happen, '...once women are allowed into the Mess. The disgusting exhibition etc.'. Despite the views of such people the WAAFs were there to stay, but tradition had to be observed. As Lianne Beauchamp, a former Section Officer in the Code and Cypher section wrote:

For the time being we were billeted in various houses in Long Bennington, ate at a separate table in the Officers' Mess, and had the use of the billiard room. We never went into the ante room except for the customary pre-Sunday lunch drinks or for mess parties. There were only six or eight of us, all in Admin., Code and Cypher and Intelligence. We kept a very low profile, and whilst I don't know how the senior

Outside the Bottesford WAAF Officers' Mess, 1942. Bunty Vardon (senior WAAF officer), Kay Kirby, Betty Davies and Lianne Beauchamp. Note the motley collection of furniture! (L. Beauchamp)

regular officers viewed this unusual state of affairs, I think the younger men enjoyed our company and we came to know many of them very well. On ordinary evenings if there were signs of a wild party brewing, Bunty Vardon, who was rather older than the rest of us, would herd us together, call for transport and we would beat a discreet retreat back to our various billets. Mine was in a big house in Long Bennington. The accommodation there was very luxurious, bedroom with bathroom en suite, all expensively carpeted, which was lovely, only I couldn't find anywhere to clean my shoes and polish my buttons!

Leading Aircraftwoman Daphne Forbes had trained as a driver (Motor Transport) at Blackpool, and Bottesford was her first posting. She recalled:

For the first few months most of us were on duty for 36 hours on and 12 hours off. This did not mean that we were driving all the time, but we were on call. Quite often I was sent off in a 15 cwt Bedford van to Worksop, Mansfield and Matlock with the airman in charge of the pigeon loft. We went mostly to miners' houses where they plied us with tea. They were kind, gentle men with such knowledge of their birds. One or two pickups were from pubs where they gave us beer and shandy. The airman in charge of the Bottesford loft was a nice bloke, who when I told him I was going on leave, said he had two awkward birds who would not return to their lofts. Before I could think straight I had two fluttering corpses in my hand. The only way to keep them was to hang them from the springs of my bed, and hope that the all-seeing Section Officer Kirby did not spot them, because the airman would have denied all knowledge, and it would have strained even my imagination to come up with a convincing story!

As well as the pigeons, we also took aircraft cylinder blocks back to Rolls-Royce, at Derby I think, for their specialist attention. We visited the armoury in the morning with boxes of ammo., took groundcrews out to bomb up in the afternoon, or drove tractors towing bomb trolleys. We carried cameras and flashes out for the camera section. There were the lorries for 'A' and 'B' Flights to carry groundcrews to dispersal points, aircrew from the messes to briefing, and later to the kites, and collect them on their return for debriefing. We also drove tractors for moving the kites, petrol bowsers, and the small ambulance. Then there were all the mundane jobs around the camp. The coal lorry visited the dispersed site, the ration waggon the Mess, salvage to the dump, mail van to the Post Office, Staff car for the CO and visiting VIPs etc. Quite a few of the older vehicles were swung started with a starting handle. They had self-starters but the batteries went flat if used too much. Because of the size of the vehicles and the muscle required to start and drive them WAAF drivers had to be over 5'4".

Our own daily routine was more or less as follows. We got up at 6 am, dressed, plodded over the ablutions hut to wash, then returned to stack blankets, biscuits (mattress) and sheets. We then tidied our bed space before getting out for working parade. We were not allowed to make our own beds until 4.30 pm. Each hut housed about 30 bods with an NCO in a small room by the entrance. We had a kit inspection, I think, about every two weeks. We had no WAAF cookhouse or NAAFI on-site at first, so we had to walk or bike to the mens' mess. Most of us missed breakfast and waited for the NAAFI waggon for 'char and a wad (a bun)'. At Bottesford one would also see a group of airmen and women standing close to the hedge opposite the farm house (Normanton Lodge), and a woman coming out with a pile of fried egg sandwiches which she had cooked to order — I think they were 6d each.

With the bad weather boredom was rife on the station, so rugby and football teams were hastily formed, resulting in an inter-flight match won by 'A' Flight. Many airmen attended carol services in Bottesford Methodist chapel, the village school and a newly opened canteen next to the green. On the 'drome itself, continuing invasion and sabotage scares led to the issue of revolvers, but despite initial enthusiasm for target practice, interest declined in proportion to a lack of results. Sergeant John Banfield, a former wireless operator recalled the furore over an article in the *Daily Mirror* which said how easy it would be for a saboteur to plant a bomb on board a bomber. Within two days Bottesford was surrounded by three coils of barbed wire!

Christmas day itself was spoilt by an order to have nine Manchesters ready for take-off at dawn to attack the *Scharnhorst* and *Gneisenau*. However, good sense prevailed and the aircraft took off instead to practice formation flying and to wish a 'Merry Christmas' to neighbouring aerodromes over the R/T. The comparative inactivity came to an end two days later when seven aircraft were readied for an attack on Dusseldorf. It was an eventful night for one crew at least. Sergeant Douglas Barnes, wireless operator on board L7483 EM-O (aptly called 'Hobson's Choice'), flown by Squadron Leader Beauchamp wrote:

One engine had failed before we reached the English coast on the way out. We dropped the bombs in the North Sea (avoiding, I hope, a convoy we were aware of) and turned back to land at Martlesham Heath. We were fired on by our own AA and then the airfield lights were lit, then extinguished. This performance was repeated several times, much to the captain's annoyance. Committed to land, we crash-landed and came far too close to a row of Spitfires as a result of the tower's games with the lights. The captain was not amused!

'Hobson's Choice' was unfortunately all too typical of its type. In the six months it had been on Squadron strength it had flown just four operations before crashing.

The start of January 1942 saw three raids in quick succession against French ports, and during an attack on Brest in the early hours of the 10th, 207 Squadron suffered its first operational loss at Bottesford, the only casualties for three months. Pilot Officer Reginald Bayley and crew in L7322 EM-Q had been the third aircraft off at 0359. The last aircraft to return landed back just after ten having been in the air for just over six hours, and whilst telephone calls from Exeter and Boscombe Down informed operations that Pilot Officers Dave Green and 'Dodo' Doble had diverted to these stations, nothing more was heard of the Bayley crew. Their Manchester had been hit by flak and crashed into the sea off the north-western coast of France. Of the seven on board four were washed ashore and buried at Crozon, but the other three are listed on the Runnymede Memorial, dedicated in 1953 to the 20,466 airmen who went missing while serving with the RAF in northern Europe during the Second World War.

After two more raids the Squadron was stood down for three days. On the 14th, despite the first fall of snow, it was called upon to join an attack on Hamburg. Modern airports have the luxury of mechanical snow clearing equipment, but at Bottesford and other aerodromes it was 'all hands to the shovels'. As parties of airmen struggled to clear roads and several thousand square yards of runway it was noticed that the Wimpey builders who had previously been much in evidence were nowhere to be seen. They were found sitting in their huts smoking, playing cards and brewing tea, lest they be roped in to the frantic activity going on around them. Their popularity had fallen since the night they had decided to dispose of some building debris on the landing ground by setting fire to it. This was bad enough, but they had chosen an air raid alert to do it in! The flames were visible for miles around, but on this occasion the Luftwaffe was slow to act and some forceful language soon ensured that the fires were dowsed. The general opinion was that since the majority of the workmen came from Eire, they had probably expected the Germans to respect their neutrality and leave well alone...

Bottesford's camouflaged technical site, February 1942. Bordered by the hangars are the main stores, the parachute store, the workshops and the squadron and flight offices — note also the crew bus. (H. Watson)

The aiming point for the crews attacking Hamburg that night was given as the dockyards and nearby Blohm und Voss aircraft factory. As it was, the North Sea was covered by a thick layer of cloud, and many aircraft were unable to locate the target. It was a particularly bad night for 207, with two aircraft failing to return. As the force droned eastwards towards the target, Manchester L7309 EM-O, skippered by Flying Officer Gerry Dawkins, was attacked by a German night fighter. Dawkins reacted quickly, throwing the aircraft into a violent turn, but although his manoeuvre shook off the fighter, they had been hit and the port engine began to surge dramatically. After a long struggle the second pilot, Flight Sergeant Geoff Allan, managed to shut it down but the propeller continued to windmill in the airflow. Although Dawkins was doing his best to maintain height, it soon became obvious that the drag was slowing them considerably and that there was no chance of reaching England. Reluctantly, they turned back towards the German coast and decided to bale out once over land. Still over the sea, everything of conceivable use to the Germans was thrown overboard, and with Dawkins holding the Manchester steady the crew prepared to leave via the escape hatch in the base of the aircraft's nose. Inexplicably, as Sergeant James Cadman knelt over the hatch, his parachute fell out through the opening. Geoff Allan immediately volunteered to carry him on his back. They were lashed together with makeshift bindings, but when the ripchord was pulled the sudden shock caused Cadman to break free and he was killed. Their aircraft crashed close to Wilhelmshaven just after nine in the evening and the six survivors were made prisoners of war.

The circumstances leading up to the loss of the second aircraft, Manchester L7523 EM-M, have never been fully established. With some sort of technical problem, Flight Sergeant Wescombe took off fifteen minutes after the rest of the Squadron. From this point nothing more was heard. His widow Audrey wrote in 1992.

For several months prior to January 1942, Basil, our daughter Marie and I shared a furnished house at 1 Harlaxton Street, Nottingham with the wireless operator, his wife Margaret, and their baby son Clemmie. We rented the house from a Mrs Cooke — she was the aunt of another member of the crew (Sergeant Westbury). The crew sometimes had nights out together in Nottingham and then had supper and spent the night in our home. Just around the corner from us there used to be what I suppose today would be called a takeaway — although customers supplied their own containers; pudding basins and old fashioned pie dishes for food such as fish and chips, faggots and peas, pie and peas and so on. The proprietors were great folk and sort of adopted 'the boys' as they called them. The boys were always great company, full of fun, never a trace of fear showing, although I know Basil knew what the odds were. Several times Basil said to me, 'Don't worry. If anything happens to me you will know'. I didn't attach any special significance to the remark until the day the crew were lost. Margaret and I had had a bad day. She kept crying for no apparent reason and things kept going wrong. It was latish in the evening before we got round to putting the little ones to bed. I went upstairs to get their nightclothes, and as I entered the bedroom I stopped. I saw Basil in a corner, at least from his hips up, wearing uniform. He was smiling, then disappeared. Imagination? No matter what anyone may say or think I know what I saw and cannot nor will not deny it.

At 20.45 farmer Walker's eldest daughter was sitting in the kitchen of Cliff House Farm in the hamlet of Holmpton on the Yorkshire coast when she heard the roar of an aircraft at extremely low level. She rushed into the yard just in time to see the aircraft pass overhead, heading inland streaming flames. Seconds later there was a flash and an explosion. Although members of the Home Guard were soon on the scene it took the Withernsea Police and the Auxiliary Fire Service over an hour to reach the crash site. They found a deep crater filled with wreckage, and propaganda leaflets printed in German were being blown about in the stiff breeze. Amongst the debris were also three bodies. The Firemen returned to their depot at 01.55 and by 02.46 it was established that the wreck was that of a British bomber. The Home Guard carried the remains of the crew to Cliff House Farm where they remained overnight before being conveyed the following morning to RAF Catfoss. The subsequent inquest held at the farm established that L7523 had jettisoned her warload out to sea, and concluded that the aircraft had probably been damaged by enemy action, forcing an early return and culminat-

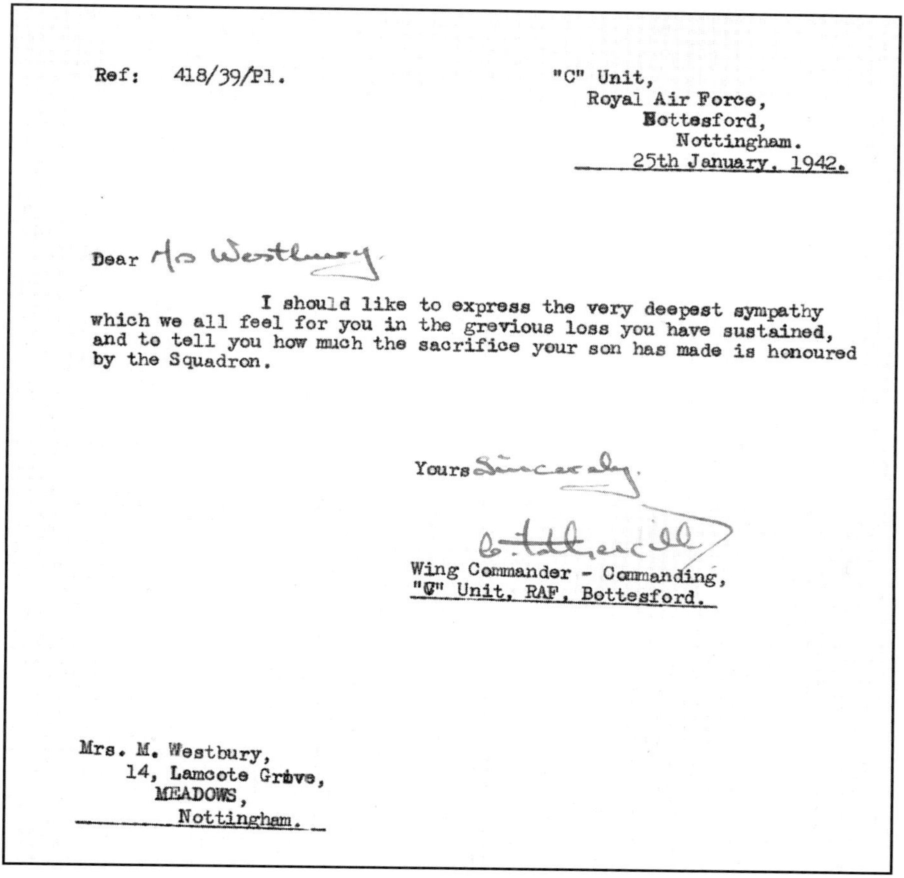

Ref: 418/39/Pl.

"C" Unit,
Royal Air Force,
Bottesford,
Nottingham.
25th January, 1942.

Dear Mrs Westbury.

I should like to express the very deepest sympathy which we all feel for you in the grevious loss you have sustained, and to tell you how much the sacrifice your son has made is honoured by the Squadron.

Yours Sincerely.

Wing Commander - Commanding,
"C" Unit, RAF, Bottesford.

Mrs. M. Westbury,
14, Lamcote Grove,
MEADOWS,
Nottingham.

Letter of condolence to Mrs Westbury of Nottingham following the loss of her son on the night of 14th January 1942.

ing in the crash. The more likely explanation given the engine fire — that failure of one of the Vultures had forced Wescombe to turn back — was apparently not considered. Such occurrences were far from unusual, and some 8,000 Bomber Command aircrew were killed in accidents over Britain in the last war. Audrey Donohue said:

I never saw Basil when my heart didn't give a skip and a jump. When he was first posted missing I dreaded the thought that perhaps he was freezing, hungry or injured in one of those yellow boats in the North Sea, so that, when I received the final telegram, although devastated, I felt a degree of relief that he wasn't suffering. This, together with the fact that his little daughter needed extra love and care helped me through those dark days.'

CHAPTER FOUR

'...a Piece of Cake'

Given the Manchester's reputation, it was with some relief that on January 16th a third flight was formed on 207 to begin converting crews onto the Lancaster. After 44 at Waddington, 207 would be only the second squadron to receive the aircraft, basically an uprated Manchester. This redesign had entailed increasing the aircraft's wingspan to incorporate the two extra powerplants and retaining the larger tail section as fitted to the last production Manchesters. Inside there were a few other differences. Most noticeable was the fact that, unlike the Manchester, the Lancaster did not have dual controls. Conversion consisted of familiarising pilots and co-pilots with slightly altered systems layouts, improved performance characteristics and new handling procedures, and was carried out on the first production Lancaster BT308. Having begun life as a Manchester, BT308 still retained its dual controls and was invaluable for initial training, although its bright yellow 'test aircraft' colour scheme presented a stark contrast to the sooty black Manchesters. The first two full production Lancasters were not delivered until the end of January, and from then on 'C' Flight's work began in earnest under the direction of Flight Lieutenant Peter Ward-Hunt, who had recently completed his second tour.

Nevertheless, if the crews thought that February was to bring them either the promise of better weather or a release from the campaign against German shipping, they were disappointed. The weather for the first few days of the month was again so bad that little flying was undertaken, but on the 4th it cleared sufficiently for three aircraft to be sent to drop mines in the shipping lanes around the Frisian Islands. Deteriorating conditions forced the crews to return early, but the fact that the operation was mounted at all indicates the seriousness with which intelligence reports were being taken, warning of the imminent break-out of the *Scharnhorst*, *Gneisenau* and *Prinz Eugen* from Brest. Like other 5 Group squadrons, 207 therefore had six Manchesters kept at permanent readiness on the rain- and windswept apron, ready fuelled and armed with 2,000 lb Armour Piercing bombs, the only ordnance likely to be able to penetrate the heavily armoured decks on the cruisers.

Over the next two weeks fog and low cloud enshrouded Bottesford, but they were still trying times for the air and ground crews kept at readiness in anticipation of a change in conditions. As it happened, 207 was not called upon until the 11th, when one crew was sent minelaying off the Frisians and six others to bomb Mannheim. Technical problems and the weather ensured that the returning aircraft were scattered across several aerodromes. Only

207 Squadron's Conversion Flight, spring 1942. F/O Dave Green (fifth left) survived the war to retire from the RAF as an Air Commodore. F/Lt Peter Ward-Hunt (fifth right) went on to become a flight commander on 106 Squadron under Guy Gibson (of Dambuster fame). (P. Ward-Hunt)

one actually managed to return to Bottesford with what were to prove unfortunate consequences, because in the early hours of February 12th the *Scharnhorst*, *Gneisenau* and *Prinz Eugen* finally slipped their moorings and headed out into the Channel under heavy escort. The same low cloud and heavy squalls which had caused problems for those attacking Mannheim provided perfect protection for the ships. The whole of 5 Group had been on four hours' readiness in anticipation of just such a turn of events, but the three cruisers were not spotted until 10.42 in the morning, and from then on the teleprinter messages flew thick and fast ordering every available aircraft into the air.

There were two problems at Bottesford. Firstly, the number of aircraft available had been reduced by the diversions the night before, and secondly, those on stand-by were still loaded with 2,000 lb Armour Piercing bombs. Since the only means of sighting the ships would be to get beneath the cloud base which extended as low as 500 feet, it was obvious that at this altitude the bombs would not gain enough velocity to pierce the armoured decks, so six aircraft were hurriedly re-loaded with twelve 500 lb General Purpose bombs apiece. The six aircraft concerned were L7455 and L7486 from the Conversion Flight, L7488 and L7432 which had been on stand-by and L7432 and L7515 which had now returned from their diversionary aerodromes. Of

F/Sgt 'Ginger' Hathersich's 'B–Beer', Manchester L7486 is refuelled at an icy West Malling on the morning of the 12th February 1942, having diverted there on return from Mannheim the night before. (Holyoak Collection)

the six L7432 and L7515, allotted to Wing Commander Fothergill and Flying Officer J.H. Leland, became unserviceable just before take-off, and Squadron Leader Thos Murray's L7485 developed a serious hydraulic leak just as he was climbing away from the aerodrome. He landed back after just seven minutes, leaving the three others to continue. Of these, Peter Ward-Hunt and Peter Birch, both instructors from the Conversion Flight, soon became lost in the impenetrable 'clag' and could not locate the ships, and only Flight Sergeant Johnny Atkinson had any luck. For a fleeting moment the clouds parted, the *Prinz Eugen* was sighted, and from only 800 feet his observer straddled the ship perfectly with his bombs. In reply they received a hit in the tail from heavy flak and limped away into the welcoming murk. The cruiser sailed on obliviously. If she was hit, the bombs had simply bounced off her deck.

Following the ineffectiveness of these attacks, a mining sortie was mounted in the evening, but the squadron was again dogged by bad luck. Of the four crews despatched only Pilot Officer Doble was able to 'sow his vegetables' successfully. Thos Murray in L7485 was unable to release his mines because of a hydraulic failure, the same ailment which had grounded him that afternoon. For the armourers it had also been a frustrating day. Some had been on duty for 48 hours, sleeping fitfully when they could, and the conflicting orders from Group with the evening's mining sortie effectively meant that the aircraft had been loaded three times in less than 24 hours. Because of mechanical faults L7485 and L7515 had been loaded, unloaded, re-loaded and then unloaded again in less than twelve hours! The one ray of light was that as the *Scharnhorst* and *Gneisenau* passed through the Frisian Islands on the final leg of their journey, both had struck air-sown mines. Although not catastrophic, this and the damage already inflicted whilst in Brest meant that they would remain inactive until further repairs were effected. Not only had they been prevented from returning to the Atlantic, but wherever they were forced to dock they would again be open to air attack.

As the snow fell on the afternoon of Saturday 21st February, 5 Group Headquarters at St.Vincents in Grantham cancelled a planned gardening sortie and the crews were gratefully stood down. However, as the evening wore on conditions improved enough for two aircraft to be readied for a smaller scale mining operation off Wilhelmshaven. Flight Sergeant Coles took off at 2038 hours, closely followed by 'Prune' Leland. Both landed back around two o'clock the following morning to report heavy icing, snow flurries and extremely poor visibility. With no horizon to guide them, flying had been on instruments, requiring intense concentration and extremely dangerous because the mines had to be dropped from 700 feet or below. At such a low altitude even a few seconds disorientation might be fatal. To make matters worse the icing made both radio communication and aircraft handling difficult. Unable to identify the target area, they had returned to Bottesford with their four 1,500 lb mines and made hazardous landings on the icy runway. Meanwhile, four other crews were anxiously waiting in the draughty Flight Office as the take-off time for their own operation was again postponed.

They had been called to readiness early the previous morning and had spent a miserable day wondering what could possibly be in store for them in such weather. They were not briefed until the afternoon, miserably tramping down to the operations block in the snow. The briefing did not cheer them any. Following the breakout from Brest the *Prinz Eugen* had sailed for Brunsbuttel from where she was ordered to Norway along with the pocket battleship *Admiral Scheer*. However, just south of Trondheim the *Prinz Eugen* had been torpedoed by the Royal Navy submarine *Trident*, forcing her to limp into a nearby fjord for repairs. The fact that the ship was now effectively trapped in the fjord made an air attack feasible, for which reason the carrier HMS *Victorious* was steaming northwards with the intention of launching her aircraft against the cruiser. The one major problem was the heavy Luftwaffe fighter presence in the area, so Bomber Command was tasked with attacking the four main German airfields. The comforting idea was that if they didn't actually succeed in destroying many fighters on the ground, they would at least create a diversion. Three 207 crews were therefore assigned to attack the Luftwaffe airfield at Sola, a mission which would be carried out at the limit of endurance for their aircraft, in appalling weather and against strong opposition.

And so they waited, anxiously peering outside and hoping for a 'scrub', but within an hour of the return of the two gardening aircraft they were at last told to prepare for take-off. Three of 207's most experienced captains had been chosen, but it had been an extremely long day, and as they reached their dispersals it began to snow again. Taxiing a fully loaded bomber in good weather was no easy matter. The long nose obscured vision and the pilot had to gun the engines and constantly fish-tail from side to side to obtain a better view as he taxied out onto the narrow perimeter track. At 0330, in a flurry of snow kicked up by his propellers, 'Dim' Wooldridge in EM-P L7484 over-corrected slightly and put a wheel off the hard standing. With full tanks and six 1,000 lb bombs on board P-Peter was stuck fast and could not be moved. Twenty-two minutes later Dave Green in K-King made a successful take-off run using the whole length of the runway, to be followed into the murk by Penny Beauchamp in B-Beer.

Things already looked grim, but the additional delay in take-off effectively meant that they would now be flying over enemy territory in daylight. It was obvious on the ground that the weather was not improving as predicted. With the continuing snowfall the crews would surely be experiencing problems with icing. The Manchesters would become heavier and the controls sloppy as the mantle of ice built up around them. Their engines would be straining with the increased load and radio contact would be lost. For this reason the recall signal was transmitted at 0500. Penny Beauchamp jettisoned his bombs and cautiously set course back to Bottesford with a frozen air speed indicator, but Dave Green's wireless operator did not receive the faint Morse signal and they carried on. However, some time later his navigator Goldie Goldstraw detected a change in wind direction, and a check on the fuel told them that they had insufficient left to attack Sola and return to Britain. They too turned back. They eventually landed back at 1024 hours, physically shattered, to discover that the attack on the *Prinz Eugen* had been a similar failure due to the appalling conditions. The one consolation was that, for once, the aircraft had held up wonderfully.

The bad luck could not last for ever and on March 3rd the Squadron was called upon to take part in a raid on the Renault works at Billancourt, to the west of Paris, where lorries were being produced for the Wehrmacht. The operation was a problematic one because although efforts could be made through the Resistance to warn workers of an impending attack, any truly effective warning would also alert the Germans. Added to this were the civilian houses which surrounded the factory. French casualties would be impossible to avoid. 207 was to provide seven crews, and the attack was to be made in three parts, flares being dropped by the first wave to clearly mark the target for those who followed. This was then a novel tactic, but its success would cause it to become widely used in the future. Two hundred and thirty five aircraft were to take part, making this the largest raid of the war so far and a turning point in the fortunes of Bomber Command. The 207 aircraft lifted off from Bottesford around six o'clock in the evening. The weather was perfect. Over France it was a clear, starry night, the River Seine shining in the strong moonlight. Sergeant George Hawes, the 26 year-old Australian second pilot on Johnny Atkinson's crew, gave a vivid account of the raid in a letter home to his parents:

It was an absolutely wizard show, and we blasted the place off the face of the map. We were the second wave to go over, and when we arrived the place was lit up by hundreds of flares and the target was a mass of flames. On the run-up we counted sixteen huge fires burning in the target area. We attacked as low as we could without getting the blast from our own exploding bombs. You can't imagine the satisfaction one gets from actually seeing your bombs land smack in the centre of the target and pieces of factory torn from the ground and thrown hundreds of feet into the air. It was the best night's work I have ever done. A great show, and as the boys say, 'a piece of cake'.

The navigator on board Peter Ward-Hunt's aircraft, Flying Officer Plaistow, had no problem identifying the target as he had worked at Billancourt before the war. As he watched the raid unfolding before him, it must have been with mixed feelings. The Renault factory was heavily damaged but French casualties were severe, proving that pin-point accuracy was still impossibly elusive.

Between the 8th and 11th March three raids were launched in as many nights against Essen, deep within Germany's heavily defended industrial heartland, the Ruhr, ironically referred to by the crews as 'Happy Valley'. On the night of the 8/9th the first of the Essen force to take off was Flight Lieutenant Peter Birch in EM-G. With him acting as observer was Group Captain Swain. Engine trouble soon forced them to abort, but Frank Roper, a good friend of Birch's recalls:

Some time during the trip Swain asked where the Elsan toilet was, and one of the smart crew members flipped on his microphone and said 'Straight down the back of the aeroplane, sir, first door on your left. Watch your step!', the step in question being 6,000 feet! We never could pin down the person who said it, it was taken as a joke anyhow, but we were pretty sure it was Sammy Hall that did it — he was that kind of guy — a fun man!

As usual, the Ruhr's notorious industrial haze made the target, the Krupps works, difficult to identify. The third raid on the night of the 10/11th March was another disappointment. Six aircraft were readied, but Ginger Hathersich's aircraft, L7455 in which Peter Birch had been forced to abort two nights before, again developed engine trouble, this time just before take-off. Of the remaining five Manchesters, Squadron Leader Beauchamp was forced to return within minutes due to failure of his port engine, and Pilot Officer John Speir RCAF returned three hours later with the same problem. This left Johnny Atkinson, 'Babe' Ruth and Frank Roper (now on his fifth operation as captain) to continue to the target. Here they found cloud, unpredicted at briefing, with the result that post-raid reconnaissance showed bombing to be extremely scattered.

When Frank Roper touched down Manchester L7485 'D-Dog' at 0330 hours on the morning of Wednesday March 11th 1942, he had completed what was to be 207 Squadron's last Manchester operation of the war. For the next few weeks the Squadron was stood down from operations whilst its crews converted on to the Lancaster. For the Manchester it was an inauspicious end to an inauspicious career, but if the aircraft exhibited one of the most dangerous characteristics of any aeroplane, mechanical unreliability, it also brought out the best in the air and ground crews who had contend with it.

F/O Frank Roper, an American in the RCAF, and Sgt 'Ham' Hamilton beneath the cavernous bomb bay of their aircraft, spring 1942. Frank Roper retired from the USAF in 1963 as a Lieutenant Colonel and Bill Hamilton ended the war as an instructor at Bottesford. (F.A. Roper)

CHAPTER FIVE

Return to Battle

For the six weeks that it was stood down 207 was busily engaged in converting on to the Lancaster. By the end of April it could boast sixteen of the new type on strength with as many trained crews. In the meantime the seemingly interminable circuits, night landings and cross-countries were not without their drama, with two aircraft being destroyed. The first and most tragic loss was that of 27-year-old Mancunian Sergeant Norman Lingard and his crew in Lancaster R5501 EM-G. Just after lunch on March 28th they were engaged in a daylight cross-country exercise south of Lincoln when Cranwell based Miles Master DK793 flown by a pupil pilot, Lieutenant Linaker, began to carry out a series of unauthorized feint attacks. Unauthorized aerobatics of any kind were expressly forbidden. Many a trainee had been killed showing off, and on one pass witnesses on the ground saw the Master slice into R5501's tail section, both aircraft spinning out of control to crash on the Bracebridge road. Lingard and fellow Sergeants Wood, Cox and Massey, along with the Master pilot were all killed instantly. Norman Lingard had already survived many operations as a second pilot and to die in such a way was particularly sad.

Fate was fortunately kinder to the crew skippered by Flight Sergeant J.J.N. McCarthy RNZAF. In the early hours of April 8th four crews were engaged in 'circuits and bumps'. A gentle rain was falling as 'Mac' McCarthy in R5498 Z-Zebra turned into the wind to line up with Bottesford's main runway. With the help of second pilot, Canadian Leo La Salle, McCarthy set the flaps fully down, lowered the undercarriage and allowed the Lancaster to sink slowly earthwards. 'Zebra' was approximately 300 feet from the end of the runway when a booster pump failed causing both starboard engines to cut out, starved of fuel. The Lancaster's airspeed fell dramatically, and she quickly began sinking and turning to starboard. As she skimmed low over the Normanton/Bennington road a wing tip struck the corner of a nearby farmhouse, Normanton Lodge, and she slewed round and 'bellied in' close by. Bruised and shaken, McCarthy, LaSalle, wireless operator John Banfield and navigator Jack Leahy rapidly scrambled clear as the wreck caught fire. The wingtip had destroyed a chimney stack and removed the corner of a bedroom, inside which was the farmer's young daughter, unharmed and miraculously still asleep! For many years afterwards the repairs to the house were visible, although when John Banfield visited the site in 1987 they could no longer be seen. A few weeks after the incident with R5498, McCarthy, indulging his passion for low flying, neatly clipped the chimney pots from the same farmhouse with his tail wheel. The first time, farmer Barnes had

Engine fitters check over the two starboard Merlins of a 207 Squadron Lancaster on its Bottesford dispersal, summer 1942. In the distance are tents belonging to an A.T.C. summer camp. (RAF Museum)

suffered the damage with reasonably good grace, but the second time around he was implacable!

207 was pronounced ready to return to 5 Group's order of battle in time for the raid on the Baltic port of Rostock on the night of the 24/25th April. Four crews took part, but whilst in the vicinity of Heligoland the rear turret on L7582 became unserviceable and Ginger Hathersich reluctantly turned back. The other aircraft found Rostock unobscured, but on their return to Britain it was a different matter altogether, and poor visibility forced two of the three to divert to Waddington and Leeming respectively. It was an inauspicious start for the Lancaster in 207's service, but the aircraft inspired confidence in a way that the Manchester never could.

When in early May Thos Murray was posted 'tour expired'[1] he was succeeded as commander of 'A' Flight by the newly promoted 'Babe' Ruth[2].

[1] Murray stayed at Bottesford and took over command of the Conversion Flight.
[2] Squadron Leader W.D.B. Ruth DFC*, MiD was to be killed on his third tour of

Although both were extremely popular, he and Ruth were as different in temperament as they were in appearance. Marie Cooper had fond memories of Ruth:

Along with his ability to command and his swift unequivocal decisions, he could just as swiftly reverse these if proved wrong. I witnessed a great performance in the Flight Office one day when he looked out of the window and saw someone make an appalling landing. 'Send that chap in!'. Before the culprit could utter a word, Ruth launched in to a tirade, tearing him off a strip with enthusiasm. When the abashed pilot had retreated, the groundcrew came in to list the series of defects the aircraft had landed with. 'Send him back in!'. On entry Ruth flung an arm around his junior's shoulder, laughing his rather high pitched laugh, and said: 'I gather I owe you an apology? Congratulations on that splendid landing you made - can't think how you did it...!'.

Through those first depressing winter months a great camaraderie had developed amongst all ranks, not least because of the aerodrome's isolated position and its lack of facilities. In the face of such adversities it was up to the men to make their own entertainment, with the result that they got to know one another much better than they might otherwise have done. For the more sedate the Officers' and Sergeants' messes had billiard and table-tennis tables, or one could sit reading, writing, or have a quiet drink in the ante room. However, on many occasions one drink would lead to another, culminating in a variety of mess games. Frank Roper remembered that favourites were 'High Cockolorum' and 'Are you there, Moriarty?'. The former involved piling furniture to the roof, and then clambering to the top, the winner being the one who could remain there. A variation on the theme was to plant sooty hand or footprints across the ceiling. Needless to say, there were frequent accidents resulting in broken limbs, and the game was later banned on RAF stations.

Not long after the crash at Fiskerton Lake in November Charles Smith had re-crewed with Pilot Officer Leland. He remembered:

Our skipper was notoriously untidy in his dress, so one night after a party in the Mess we persuaded him to let us press his uniform in our room. After completing the job and several more drinks, he was about to set off to his own room on the other side of the airfield when it began to pour down with rain. Not wishing to get his freshly pressed uniform wet he insisted on wrapping it up in brown paper to keep it dry. Having done this he set off in the pouring rain dressed only in his underwear. Unfortunately he fell in a ditch, lost his uniform and arrived at his quarters soaking wet and covered in mud. He alerted the Guard Room to find his uniform — which they did the next morning. So much for our efforts to smarten up our skipper!'

operations on June 12th 1944 flying with 201 Squadron. He is commemorated on the Runnymede Memorial.

As a postscript to the story, having fallen in the ditch, Leland had apparently decided to make his way back to the Mess for a stiff drink. Unbeknown to him, several of the WAAF officers who had attended the party were still waiting for transport to take them back to their billets. Just as they were preparing to leave, the pilot burst in, soaking, and clad only in his air force issue long johns. With great presence of mind the senior WAAF officer, Bunty Vardon, seized a nearby greatcoat and hurriedly wrapped it around him to spare the blushes of her charges!

The railway line running through Bottesford offered access to the pubs and cinemas of Grantham or Nottingham. There was also a regular bus service but this was generally shunned by the WAAF's wishing to avoid the attentions of the amorous builders who were still working on the aerodrome. Nottingham's most famous attractions were The Trip to Jerusalem, The Flying Horse (or Airborne Nag) and the Black Boy, and for those who liked dancing and the girls, The Palais de Danse - all well known to Bomber Command. Closer to home, Bottesford had The Red Lion (officers only) and the Bull's Head. The latter was used by airmen and had the distinction of being run by Stan Laurel's sister. In Foston there was the Black Boy, another regular haunt, and even more popular (because they could be reached via Sewstern Lane without going past the Service Police) were Long Bennington's The Reindeer and the Wheatsheaf. Others might take a bus to Newark, strike out on their bicycles deep into the Vale of Belvoir or perhaps hitch a lift on one of the many trucks travelling through Bennington on the A1.

The preferred form of transport for Sergeant Doug Barnes was a basic £3.19.9d model Royal Enfield bicycle, bought for him with the help of his aunt and uncle who lived in nearby Foston. He remembered that his disgust knew no bounds when he arrived back at Bottesford station after a day in Nottingham to discover that his bike had been stolen in preference to more expensive models! AC2 Dennis Bentley cycled to Nottingham whenever he could, and on the one occasion he did use the train he was picked up by the M.P.s on Nottingham Low Level station for wearing his hat 'contrary to King's regulations' (it was in his pocket). When there were no passes available, the more daring airmen would exchange their gum boots for shoes, sneak across the boundary hedge and hitch to Nottingham. On their return the following morning they would smear their faces with a little grease or oil to pretend they had been working through the night, forge a late breakfast 'chit' and take their place in the dining hall. Food was relatively plentiful on the station, but because of the thousands of meals that had to be prepared every day, presentation sometimes left a lot to be desired. For this reason anything to supplement the rations was eagerly sought after. One armourer was encouraged by his hut companions to court a particularly unattractive farmer's daughter because of her ready supply of fresh bread and eggs. His protests led to calls for him to remember where his loyalties were!

The poor facilities available on a temporary aerodrome in comparison to the more comfortable pre-war examples made men go to great lengths to escape whenever possible. AC2 Ernie Spooner, an armourer from Nottingham, particularly recalled the resourcefulness of one groundcrew NCO, a Flight Sergeant who built a concealed tank in the roof of his car designed to hold surreptitiously obtained aviation fuel. He would start the car on rationed petrol and then using a special tap, switch to 100 Octane, accompanied by much spluttering, banging and backfiring. By this method he commuted to and from his married quarters in Waddington and avoided spending off-duty hours at Bottesford. In the end he burned out his valves but preserved some semblance of marital bliss!

For airmen, opportunities for unwinding on the station were far more limited. Their socializing had to be done in the Y.M.C.A. next to the Airmens' Mess, which contained a bar, a billiard room and a canteen. They could also attend filmshows in the station gymnasium, or the periodic shows put on by ENSA, the services' concert party (unkindly referred to as 'Every Night Something Awful'). One unexpected source of entertainment concerned charges of indecency brought against the Station Warrant Officer, the unfortunate man standing accused of propositioning an orderly in the sick quarters. SWO's were generally not liked by airmen, because a major part of their responsibility was to enforce discipline and dispense punishment. A former Sergeant on 207 Squadron takes up the story:

The Court had assembled and the Defending and Prosecuting Officers had been called, the prisoner was called, and the Court Orderly went to the door and bellowed at the top of his voice, 'Members of the Public'. All the 'erks' in Bottesford, or it seemed like all of them, tried to stampede through the door to witness the downfall of the Station Warrant Officer. They didn't all get in, as it was quite a small courtroom. I seem to remember I was there, I must have been officiating in some way. The outcome was that he went down for twelve months hard labour, but the evidence which his 'victim' gave was quite amusing. He was asked firstly, 'Had the Station Warrant Officer's attentions been forced on him?' 'Oh no', he said, 'I was quite willing'. 'Why, then, did you eventually complain about this?' Addressing the Court, he said, 'Well sir, I didn't mind his attentions during duty hours, but he wanted me on my days off, and I thought that a bit much!'.

The room temporarily dissolved into uproar...

On the night of 22/23rd May the 'B' Flight commander, Penny Beauchamp and his crew in Lancaster R5499 EM-O took part in a very eventful mining sortie. Flying with him as second pilot was the Squadron commander, Charles Fothergill. The Beauchamp crew were briefed to lay their mines in the Fehrmarn Belt of islands, codenamed 'Willows', and took off at 2152 hours. The operation went smoothly until the port-outer engine stopped whilst the aircraft was still off Aero Island. The mines were therefore jettisoned 'safe' and Beauchamp set course back to England. In the clear conditions he decided it was prudent to keep as low as possible to avoid detection. As 'O-Orange' thundered over the Danish coast north east of Ringkjobing, tracer suddenly flashed towards them and they were fixed by searchlights.

Already low, the Lancaster struck the water a glancing blow as Beauchamp was temporarily blinded. He reacted quickly and hauled back on the control column. By now they had only two good engines, one with a buckled propeller. The navigator, Douglas Barnes remembered looking on in surprise as sea water shorted out his Gee navigation set and started an electrical fire, also putting out of action both the IFF device and the radios. The crew prepared for ditching, but by jettisoning everything removable they managed to gain just a little height and hover above stall speed. 'Orange' limped slowly westwards to cross the east coast at a little under 700 feet. She touched down at Bottesford at 0417 hours after a feat of outstanding airmanship.

Whilst the drama was unfolding, Squadron Leader Beauchamp's wife Lianne, a WAAF officer in Code and Cypher, was at home asleep. They had met at Bottesford, and in April had asked Group Captain Swain for permission to marry. As Lianne Beauchamp wrote:

It all happened so quickly, like a dream. We were engaged on the Friday and married by special licence on the following Wednesday, for we only had ten days leave. Before leaving we had fixed up accommodation in Long Bennington. I no longer remember the name of the dear lady who let the rooms to us, but I do remember the huge bunch of golden daffodils she thrust into my arms as we drove off in 'Pen's' little Morris Eight open tourer on that glorious spring morning, with not a care in the world!

Unusually for the services they were allowed to remain together on the station, and on nights when her husband was flying Lianne Beauchamp often slept in the WAAF Mess, keeping well away from operations. When the aircraft were due back she would sometimes assemble with the other WAAFs in Bunty Vardon's room, mug of cocoa in hand, to listen on the wireless for the returning crews. After debriefing and breakfast, Squadron Leader Beauchamp would collect his wife from the Mess, by climbing through a window and carrying her back to his car. He was surprised one morning on doing this to see the headlights pointing heavenwards. The mystery was soon solved when he got closer and discovered he'd forgotten to put the handbrake on and the Morris had rolled backwards into a ditch. However, on the night that he got into difficulties over Denmark, his wife had gone back to their rented rooms in Long Bennington at 'Quettadene', and the first that she knew of the incident was when he woke her at seven. Sergeant Scotty Scott, a wireless operator with 207, had this to say of the incident:

When out mine laying, which was a fairly low-level business, crews used to come back and say 'We got seaweed in the bomb bay'. Similar lines were constantly shot. On this occasion, when Beauchamp got back to Bottesford he was asked how he made out. He said 'Some people say they had seaweed in the bomb doors, but go and have a look for yourself...!'.

The training of crews had to be a continual process, either to make good operational losses or to replace those few lucky enough to finish their tour of

S/Ldr 'Penny' Beauchamp undergoing conversion at the controls of the first production Lancaster, BT308, February 1942. Events in May were to prove his mastery of the aircraft. (P. Ward-Hunt)

operations. At this stage of the war a pilot would still have to serve a long apprenticeship as second pilot before becoming captain of his own aircraft. Because throughout 1942 escalating losses were placing a serious drain on trained pilots, it was decided that the post of second pilot on heavy bombers would be replaced by that of Flight Engineer. These were to be technically minded men whose task was to assist in monitoring instruments and fuel, effect minor repairs in the air, and as a last resort take over from a wounded

S/Ldr Penny Beauchamp and crew, April 1942. Left to right: Sgt Martin, Sgt Chiasson, Sgt Paul, S/Ldr Beauchamp, P/O Oliver, Sgt Barnes, Sgt Whiteman. Tom Paul was injured soon afterwards whilst training as a first pilot. (K.H.P. Beauchamp)

pilot. They were easier to train than pilots, but would not begin reaching squadrons in any numbers until the end of 1942. Until then, for every single crew missing, two pilots would be lost.

In a strange quirk of fate, the day after Penny Beauchamp's fine effort with R5499, his former second pilot, Sergeant Tom Paul RNZAF was badly injured in an accident whilst training with his new crew. They had been sent on a night cross-country exercise over Wales and the south-west in Lancaster R5617. Unfortunately the weather deteriorated to such an extent that the recall signal was transmitted. Faced with a rapidly advancing weather front, the inexperienced Paul elected to try and avoid the worst effects of the storm by getting beneath the cloud base rather than climbing above it. In order to minimise the risk of colliding with high ground, it was standard procedure to fly well out to sea before beginning a descent in poor visibility. The crew probably believed they were over water, but at 2330 hours their Lancaster emerged from the murk and struck Standon Hill on the edge of Dartmoor. It disintegrated on impact, killing the second pilot Andrew Paterson and three others instantly. Tom Paul received severe head injuries, but the wireless operator, Sergeant Tom Whiteman miraculously escaped with only minor cuts and bruises. Fifty years on, the only local memories of the night R5617 crashed were of a Tavistock smallholder finding one of the crew's watches. For Tom Paul luck was to remain elusive. He recovered, only to be killed in January 1944 in another accident.

CHAPTER SIX

Operation Millennium

As the groundcrews made their way out to the flights after breakfast on the 30th May, it was with the knowledge that they had a very long day ahead of them. For one thing, since the 26th May the number of aircraft to be readied every morning was almost double they had been asked to prepare before. Something special appeared to be in the offing. Successes were desperately needed, something very much in the mind of the Command's CO, Sir Arthur Harris. Since Harris had taken over Bomber Command in February major strides forward had been made in both techniques and results, but many still doubted its effectiveness. Harris knew that something was required which would fire the imagination of the public, whilst at the same time demonstrating the potential of strategic bombing and silencing its detractors. This led him to suggest to Churchill and Sir Charles Portal, the Chief of the Air Staff, the idea of a single raid on a German city using 1,000 aircraft, and just as he'd hoped, the idea was an appealing one. But agreement did not alter the fact that the operation would be supremely difficult to plan, and also a major gamble.

Although the Billancourt raid back in March had introduced the idea of a concentration of aircraft making synchronous bombing runs over the target, the new plan called for three times as many aircraft. This would greatly increase the chances of collision. And what if, rather than swamping the defences as hoped, the concentration merely made the aircraft easy targets? Even more important was the fact that Bomber Command lacked the resources to make such an attack. It would be necessary to use crews from Operational Training Units, and whilst these would include experienced instructors, many would be untried. The potential for disaster was certainly there. Harris hoped to use the force towards the end of May when there would be a full moon. As it turned out, poor weather delayed the raid and forced a change in target from the Germany's second largest city, Hamburg, to its third, Cologne.

From the moment the teleprinter clattered into life in the operations block around midday on May 30th, the excitement began to build. In the early afternoon the details came through. Bottesford was required to provide twelve aircraft. Briefing was at 6.30. When Group Captain Swain announced that the force would comprise over one thousand aircraft, making this the largest raid in the history of air warfare, there were spontaneous cheers and shouts of approval. A personal message from Sir Arthur Harris concluded the briefing, 'Let him have it — right on the chin!'. As the crews trudged up

Lancaster R5632 'N–Nuts' of 207 Squadron and its crew on dispersal, Bottesford summer 1942. (C. Hawes)

to the communal site they were in good humour. The noise from the Sergeants' Mess following the pre-ops meal made a sharp contrast to the normal subdued conversation before take-off as the men stood in groups, laughing together and singing all the ribald songs in their repertoire. The singing and cat-calls continued as lorries took them down onto the airfield to dress for the flight ahead.

By midnight all were in their aircraft carrying out final checks. Just two days before Wing Commander F.R. Jeffs AFC had taken over command of the Squadron from Charles Fothergill. Not yet checked out on the Lancaster himself, he now stood by the aerodrome control van watching the aircraft taxi out for take-off. All twelve lifted off safely in the space of thirteen minutes. A part of the third and final wave, by the time they reached Eindhoven seventy miles from the target, the attack had already begun and Cologne was visible as a bright glow on the horizon. There was no cloud and good visibility, but a dense swathe of smoke reached up to over 15,000 feet over the city. The flak defences appeared to be overwhelmed and searchlights listlessly swept the skies. All the crews from Bottesford reported that they had bombed the 'primary' aiming point, and the journeys to and from the target were described as uneventful, although 'Prune' Leland spotted a Ju 88 which did not attack, and an engine failed on 'Mac' McCarthy's aircraft. He flew back on three engines, well within the Lancaster's capabilities. Numerous bombers had been seen falling in flames. Bomber Command lost 41 aircraft, considered an acceptable proportion given the number actually taking part and the damage inflicted. Flight Sergeant Bobby Weatherall, a Canadian air gunner on 'Pat' Pattinson's crew wrote in his diary:

Twelve-thirty finds us leaving the English coast. Climbed to 13,000 feet where it was minus 20 degrees. Quiet trip all the way in, and I had a sore neck looking for fighters that weren't there. Well, it is inhumanly impossible to imagine what a sight met us. The second (sic) largest city in Germany bust and shattered. The city looked like one huge bonfire. We ran in and dropped our load. I saw the 4,000 lbs go, and what a sight! Steered a course for home; they were after us all the way back. Ric got sick from weaving.

Harris was not slow to capitalize on the success of his gamble which had captured newspaper headlines across the world. Two nights later on the night of 1/2nd June he organized another outing for the force, this time to Essen in the Ruhr. A new record of fourteen crews from 207 were detailed. Take-off was just before midnight, but in the event four aircraft were forced to return early, three with engine failure and the last with a malfunction in the oxygen system. For those who reached the target visibility was reduced by cloud and industrial haze. The Wellingtons of 3 Group had been tasked with dropping marker flares whilst the crews from Bottesford were a part of the 5 Group follow-up, their job to stoke up the fires. To this end each aircraft carried a 4,000 lb 'cookie' packed with high explosive, and also canisters containing 720 4 lb incendiaries. For official purposes this combination of weaponry was chillingly described as 'Blast and Maximum Incendiary': the cookie would tear open buildings and the incendiaries would burn whatever was exposed. Because the raid had not gone to plan Essen was again the target on the 2/3rd. Six aircraft from 207 took part, and Bobby Weatherall, again flying with 'Pat' Pattinson wrote:

Briefed at 6.30 and once more it was Essen. Bang on feed in the Mess. Took off at 12 and headed out. Passed out from lack of oxygen but came around again O.K. again, it is up to us to light the fires. Feeling very bad. Two motors conked out, but we made it on the other two. Landed at base in good time. Went straight on leave.'

As Weatherall headed off on leave preparations were being made for a raid that night on Bremen. With no cloud to hamper them, the force inflicted heavy damage on the city. Unfortunately Warrant Officer Colin Wathey and crew in EM-Y R5847 became the Squadron's first Lancaster casualties when they were shot down over the Netherlands by a nightfighter. All seven were killed. The Squadron had not lost a crew on operations for four months, but these were to be the first of a steady run which would continue for another three years. By the end of the war 207 Squadron would have the second highest loss rate in the whole of 5 Group with 926 aircrew killed.

Bottesford was closed to flying on Monday 15th June whilst arrester gear was fitted at each end of the three runways. This was an adaptation of the equipment used on aircraft carriers and was designed to prevent accidents caused by bombers making delayed touchdowns and overshooting. Many Manchester captains preferred to make powered approaches, considering it better to make a fast landing with speed in hand rather than risk having to open up and go round again — which, given the nature of the Vulture, was always a gamble. The equipment, manufactured by Mather and Platt Ltd of Manchester, consisted of a large brake drum around which was wrapped a steel hawser. This ran from the drum through a series of pulleys across the runway and back again, then on to another drum, the cable being raised to a height of 12 inches. The aircraft were to be fitted with hydraulically operated hooks with which to 'snag' the wire, and tests on the Manchester indicated that it could be brought to a halt from a speed of 72 mph in a distance of 460 yards. The installation of arrester gear was calculated at £21,000 per airfield, roughly £350,000 in today's money. However, by the time tests had been completed and the arrester gear installed at twenty aerodromes, pilot training had been improved, runways generally lengthened and the weight penalty brought about by the attachment of hooks to aircraft was considered too much. More importantly, Manchesters had been phased out from operations. The scheme was therefore officially discontinued in June 1943, and at Bottesford the mechanisms were never used operationally. Very astutely, George Hawes had noted in his diary:

They are putting in 'arrester' gear at the end of each runway. I am wondering if this great added expense is really worthwhile and what is going to happen to all this equipment after the war is finally over. I'm tipping it will just be left to rot like thousands of pounds worth of other material...

As predicted, heavily rusted but otherwise intact, the arrester units still remain *in situ* today. However, at about the same time as the arrester gear was fitted, surface cracks and sinkage began to appear on both the runways and perimeter tracks. The problems were attributed to subsidence, possibly due to an underground stream. They underlined the difficulties of having to build so many airfields at once, in that a lack of suitable sites inevitably led to the use of locations which might otherwise have been rejected. As an example, Bottesford's shortest runway, 09/27 always had a noticeable hump in the middle. Hurried plans were made for resurfacing, and because there was no other aerodrome locally which could take the Squadron, it remained operational whilst the work went on around it. In the short term crews only flew from other aerodromes when repairs forced the closure of a particular runway. As it turned out, the temporary closure of sections of the peri-track was to have dire consequences.

As part of a continuing campaign against the city, the port of Emden on Germany's north eastern coast received attention on the night of the 20th June. Thirteen 207 crews were to take part, one being scrubbed before take-off. Three others returned early due to mechanical problems, a higher number than usual since generally 207 had one of the best serviceability rates in the

The remains of the arrester gear alongside Bottesford's main runway today. The two cable drums protrude from their water filled pit, with — to the right — the control panel. (W.R. Baguley)

Group. However, if these crews thought they had problems, Flight Lieutenant Gerry Ings would surely have swapped places with them. An hour after leaving Bottesford both starboard engines failed and caught fire, forcing him to ditch Lancaster R5860 EM-Y in the North Sea. The wireless operator's last transmission at 0053 gave their position as fifty miles off the Lincolnshire coast. When the last 207 aircraft touched down three hours later there was no more news of Ings. Although tired, after debriefing the crews asked Wing Commander Jeffs for permission to go back out and search for the popular Londoner and his crew. Much to their disgust 'Ferdie' Swain vetoed the idea, but a 1 Group Wellington found them in their dinghy after first light and they returned to Bottesford, battered but unbowed.

CHAPTER SEVEN

'Yours in memory'

For several weeks 5 Group crews had been practising low level formation flying for what was to be another of Bomber Command's forays into daylight operations. Section Officer Marie Cooper flew with the crews on training flights whenever the opportunity arose, and her unofficial logbook records an entry which casts an interesting light on the preparations for the raid. The entry, headed 'Low Level Formation Flying Practice' reads:

4.05 hours with Flight Lieutenant Ings. Very lively. Birds fell off trees, ducks ran into ponds etc.

Flight Lieutenant S.E. 'Pat' Pattinson recalled:

The most terrible briefing we had was 11th July 1942 — we were told we were going on a daylight raid. We went into the crew room to wait for the briefing — we thought we would pull a few legs you see! We put in a course to Hamburg in daylight, we thought that would shake the boys, all sitting back rather complacently. The Duty Officer came in and said 'Who's the optimist?'. It was actually Danzig!

The planned attack on the U-Boat yards at Danzig in Poland would entail a round trip of 1,500 miles, the deepest penetration yet undertaken by Bomber Command and, because of the short summer nights, it was obvious that the raid could not be made in darkness. The plan therefore called for the aircraft to take off in daylight, form up in 'Vee' formation, and set course over the North Sea at low level. In this way they would not appear on German radar until the last possible minute, and if attacked, would be better able to protect each other. Predicted cloud over Denmark would shield them as they gained height for the final leg of the journey and began their runs. Around five o'clock that Saturday afternoon ten Lancasters led by Wing Commander Jeffs took off in quick succession and, circling overhead, formed up and set course eastwards. Unfortunately, before long cloud and drizzle began to make formation flying difficult, and afraid of collisions, they went their separate ways, anxiously straining their eyes in the gloom. Sergeant Peter Rae, the 21-year-old Glaswegian mid-upper gunner on Arthur Read's crew vividly remembered flying for hours in the 'clag' before suddenly emerging into a vast amphitheatre between cloud banks. Briefly, he saw another Lancaster ahead of them in the distance before it disappeared into a magnificent white wall of cloud. This was the only other aircraft they had seen, and since they

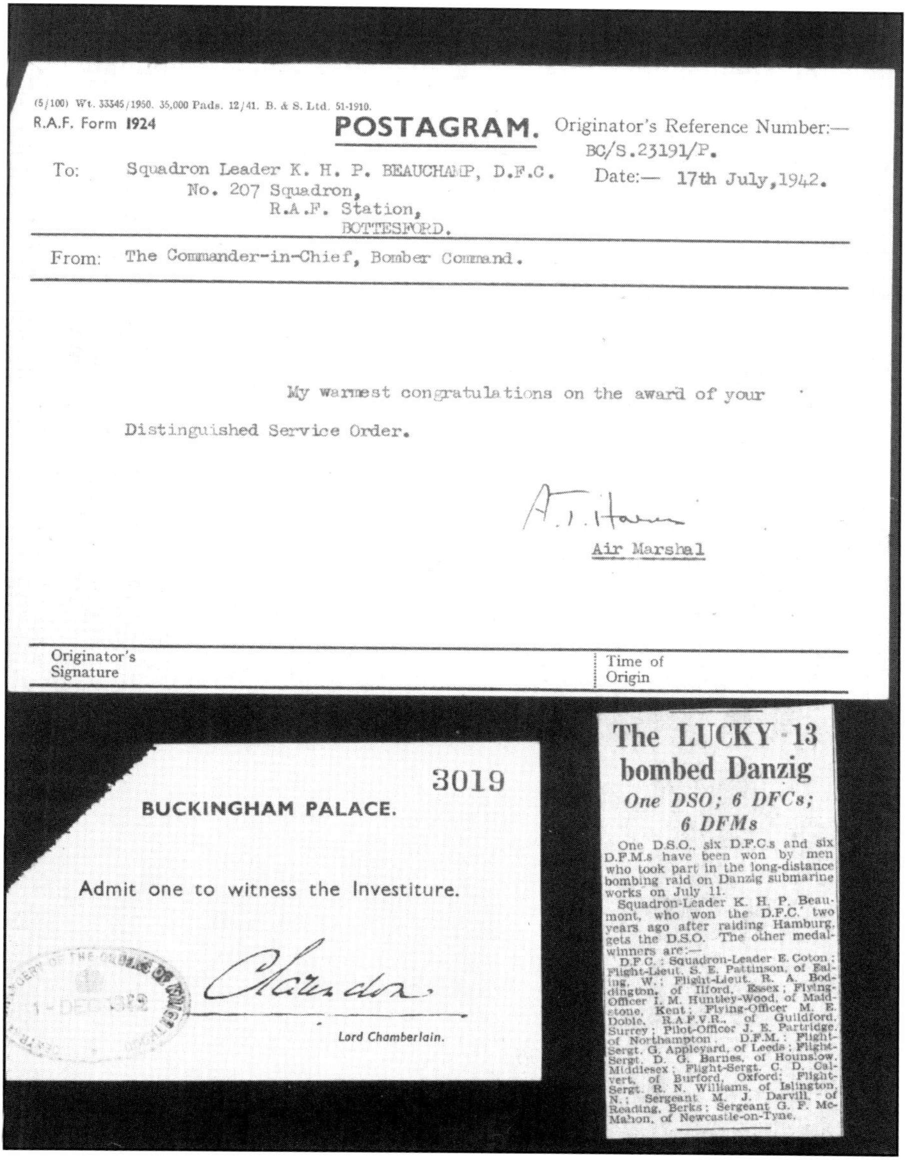

(5/100) Wt. 33345/1950. 35,000 Pads. 12/41. B. & S. Ltd. 51-1910.
R.A.F. Form 1924

POSTAGRAM.

Originator's Reference Number:— BC/S.23191/P.

Date:— 17th July, 1942.

To: Squadron Leader K. H. P. BEAUCHAMP, D.F.C.
No. 207 Squadron,
R.A.F. Station,
BOTTESFORD.

From: The Commander-in-Chief, Bomber Command.

My warmest congratulations on the award of your Distinguished Service Order.

A. T. Harris
Air Marshal

Originator's Signature | Time of Origin

3019

BUCKINGHAM PALACE.

Admit one to witness the Investiture.

Clarendon
Lord Chamberlain.

1 - DEC 1942

The LUCKY 13 bombed Danzig

One DSO; 6 DFCs; 6 DFMs

One D.S.O., six D.F.C.s and six D.F.M.s have been won by men who took part in the long-distance bombing raid on Danzig submarine works on July 11.

Squadron-Leader K. H. P. Beaumont, who won the D.F.C. two years ago after raiding Hamburg, gets the D.S.O. The other medal-winners are:—

D.F.C.: Squadron-Leader E. Coton; Flight-Lieut. S. E. Pattinson, of Ealing, W.; Flight-Lieut. R. A. Boddington, of Ilford, Essex; Flying-Officer I. M. Huntley-Wood, of Maidstone, Kent; Flying-Officer M. E. Doble, R.A.F.V.R., of Guildford, Surrey; Pilot-Officer J. E. Partridge, of Northampton. D.F.M.: Flight-Sergt. G. Appleyard, of Leeds; Flight-Sergt. D. G. Barnes, of Hounslow, Middlesex; Flight-Sergt. C. D. Calvert, of Burford, Oxford; Flight-Sergt. R. N. Williams, of Islington, N.; Sergeant M. J. Darvill, of Reading, Berks; Sergeant G. F. McMahon, of Newcastle-on-Tyne.

A page from the scrapbook of (the then) S/Ldr K.H.P. Beauchamp showing a result of the difficult Danzig raid of 11/12th July 1942; gallantry awards for members of 207 and the other squadrons taking part, including a well deserved DSO for Beauchamp. (K.H.P. Beauchamp) had lost their leader and were unsure of their position they decided to turn back, as did four others. Frank Roper, flying EM-H recalled:

Formation flying was impossible. We started out with ten aircraft flying low, below 10,000 feet, and out over the North Sea we got down to 100 feet or less. But it was just impossible to fly formation at that level with miserable weather and miserable visibility, so the formation just kind of broke up. I elected to go up to a higher altitude to see if we could get above it. By the time we got to Denmark we were at something like between 10–12,000 feet, and all of a sudden everything opened up, there was a big clear area, and we could clearly see the airport at Flensburg, and could see fighters taking off. At that point we headed for Sweden, and on the way joined a five plane V-formation from another squadron. Very shortly we ran into a cloud bank, and when we came out the other side we were in the No.2 position on the left instead of the No.5 position on the right! That was enough to tell us there was no sense trying to fly any kind of formation...

Bobby Weatherall wrote in his diary:

Had dinner and am told we are doing a daylight raid. Briefed at two, and what a trip! Formed up and away we went. Plenty of cloud at first and then bright sunshine. About half an hour out we really ran into it. Rain and thunderstorms came our way from then on. Hit our target in bright sunshine, and then it happened. Ran in at 6,000 feet and they really shot hell out of us. I thought my time had come. Dropped our bomb load smack on them, and then put the nose down to the tune of 330 mph. Same trip back — rain and lightning. Got back at 2.30 am. We were up for a stretch of ten hours. One crew is missing, although four of us got to the target from here. Had supper, then down to my bunk to thank God for a safe return.

As Weatherall remarked, the flak had been murderous, but despite the fierce opposition only two of the 44 Lancasters taking part were lost, both over the target area. One of them was 207's Z-Zebra piloted by 26-year-old Flight Sergeant George Duke. As a postscript to this raid, a party had been organized in the Sergeants' Mess for that Saturday evening, and knowledge of this prompted Peter Rae and fellow crew members to exhort their skipper to 'stuff the nose down' to get back in time for the festivities. They landed at 2121, and following debriefing hurried up to the Mess still in flying boots, only to discover that the party was all but over. Their disappointment was slightly tempered by the fact that the female guests seemed to find their attire appealing, and they were soon surrounded by eager WAAFs!

The early hours of July 22nd 1942 saw the first of three raids in quick succession on Duisberg in the Ruhr Valley. The crews were again briefed for Duisberg on the afternoon of the 23rd, take-off being set for the early hours of the following morning. However, Duisberg was shielded by cloud and the bombing poor. Five aircraft failed to return out of the 215 taking part, only two of them Lancasters, both ironically from 207 Squadron. Even more ironic was the fact that they were flown by two very good friends, 'Mac'

The crew of F/Sgt George Hawes RAAF, June 1942. Left to right: 'Bill' Blair, Percy Hooper, Frank Clarke, Eric Cartwright, Bill Smith and George Hawes. (C. Hawes)

McCarthy and George Hawes. McCarthy's R5867 T-Tommy crashed at Baerl on the Dutch-German border and the crew were buried together at Krefeld. Just days before, McCarthy's mid-upper gunner Flight Sergeant 'Roger' Rowland had made a special trip back to his home town, Leicester, to collect the engagement ring which he had intended to give to his girlfriend.

George Hawes's R5632 N-Nuts was never seen again. Six of the crew are commemorated on the Runnymede Memorial. The seventh, the 33-year-old Canadian bomb aimer Flight Sergeant T.C. Blair was washed ashore near Amsterdam on October 12th. 'Bill' Blair's sense of humour made him an extremely popular man, and he became a good friend of the Doubleday family in Bottesford village. He was a teetotaller and liked to sit with the Doubledays quietly reading, finding that this helped to ease the homesickness. Arthur Doubleday was the village builder and undertaker and the Hawes crew joined him in worship at the Methodist church whenever possible. They were also honoured guests at the wedding of his son. The poignant last letter written by Bill Blair to his family was characteristically simply but eloquently put:

Dear ones at home,

This letter I will leave in my locker and will only be posted if I don't come back from one of these raids...

At home there are all of you, thinking, working and praying that this war will end and that Gilbert and I will both come home to you. You are all playing as great a part as we are in this struggle of humane against the inhuman. When here, so far away from home and with considerable leisure time, one lives as much in the past as possible and as little in the future. In times like these I am very glad Mother for having been raised in a good Christian home and I am more than glad for my temperate habits. When I go out on these trips I think of what Dad said when he was at the end of his journey — 'Don't cry boys, take good care of your mother and Alice'. To this I add, your wives and wee ones; and remember whatever price I pay, I gladly pay, so that you may be happy and free.

Yours in memory
Clayton.

As a tragic footnote Bill's brother Gilbert was killed a year later in the Italian campaign. Bobby Weatherall's own flight that night with 'Pat' Pattinson had been cancelled due to magneto trouble. When he learned that his friends 'Mac' McCarthy, Bill Blair and George Hawes had failed to return he was devastated. He wrote in his diary:

24th July
Woke at 6 and saw George wasn't back. After that I slept fitfully until 11 when the Station Police woke me and told me that George and Mac had not come back. I was stunned by the news; it couldn't be. All my pals wiped out in one night. Gathered up George's personal belongings. Went up to the Mess and had dinner but couldn't eat. I prayed to God that they are safe and sound. I'll pay them back twice over for this.'

25th July
I'd like to leave this page blank in memory of some great fellows, George, Bill and Mac, who all lived with me at some time or another. And to Percy (Hooper) and Leo (La Salle) and the rest of the fellows who I was proud to call my friends. We can only hope that you are prisoners, but in either case I'll carry on and do my best to drop enough bombs to wreck Jerry for a long time... So cheerio fellows and keep plugging...

Bobby Weatherall went on to complete a second tour before being killed in 1944, aged just 23. He left a wife in Canada whom he had not seen since he embarked for England in 1941. The fate of these four friends epitomises the sacrifices of those from the 'Dominions'.

Although August 1942 was a terrible month for casualties, Wednesday/Thursday 5/6th stood out as the worst single night. The veteran Ings crew were shot down by a nightfighter over Holland whilst returning from an attack on Essen. Ings had had a lucky escape when forced to ditch a Lancaster back in June, but in the meantime he had married, and Marie Cooper remembered being given the task of going to the hotel where he and his bride were staying in order to break the unhappy news that he was required for 'ops' that night. Her guilt for disturbing the happy couple was doubled when Ings was killed.

Three Amigos! Canadian F/Sgts Bob Weatherall and 'Bill' Blair (in 'tycoon' guise) with F/Sgt George Hawes RAAF. As his diary entries show, Bob Weatherall was hit hard by the death of his hut companions. (C. Hawes)

However, this was not all. Whilst some crews were on the Essen raid, several others new to the squadron were engaged in practice flights in the circuit. At five minutes past midnight on the morning of August 6th, Lancaster R5550 flown by Sergeant F.S. Akerman landed, and because of repairs being undertaken on the perimeter track, was ordered by Flying Control to taxi back down the runway in use. Meanwhile, thinking that Akerman was already clear, permission was given for Manchester L7385 to land on the same runway. The two aircraft met head-on, there was an explosion, and although both the ambulance and fire tender raced to the scene, four aircrew had died instantly. A fifth died minutes later in the arms of the Medical Officer, Alan Ambrey-Smith. Amongst the dead were Frederick Akerman, pilot of the Lancaster and his flight engineer, who were both buried at St. Mary's, Bottesford.

Miraculously, five crewmen had escaped from the collision alive, although with varying degrees of injury. The pilot of the Manchester, 20-year-old Sergeant Arthur Pearson, was admitted to the Burns Unit at the RAF hospital at Rauceby. He later returned to flying, but not operationally. Flight Sergeant Dick Ikin, sitting in the rear turret of the Lancaster suffered shock and concussion. His only recollection of the accident was of waking up briefly in the ambulance and seeing another airmen whose face was covered in blood, at which point he passed out again. Sent home to Brighton to convalesce, he stayed out later than usual one night and decided to catch a bus home. Unfortunately the driver was having none of it, and declared 'This bus is for war-workers only!'. Dick Ikin's reply is not recorded...

By rights, Sergeant 'Scotty' Scott should have been with Dick Ikin on board the Lancaster that night. He had joined 207 in November 1940 as a Wireless Operator/Air Gunner, and having lost his original crew early on, had flown as a 'spare' before being re-crewed with Akerman in July. However, since Akerman's bomb aimer Sergeant Smart had originally trained as a wireless operator himself, he and Scotty decided that they would take it in turns to fly when on local exercises. With a night off, Scotty therefore got on his bicycle and rode off to Newark for the evening. He knew nothing of the incident until the next morning, when entering the 'C' Flight office to see if he was needed, Thos Murray looked up, surprised, and exclaimed, 'What the hell are you doing here? You should be dead!'. Scotty has often reflected since what a wonderful greeting that was!

Five nights after the collision on the runways Flying Officer Speir and crew were lost without trace whilst carrying out a gardening sortie in the Kattegat. On the 12/13th the aircraft of Flight Sergeant Kane and Sergeant Fry failed to return. Four nights later it was Pilot Officer Southwell and Flight Sergeant Sutherland who went missing. Southwell in R5616 EM-J was shot down by a fighter off the coast of Denmark. One crew member, Sergeant Read, was brought ashore injured but the other six were killed. Anthony Southwell's pregnant wife lived in rented accommodation in Bottesford village, a practice which was officially discouraged but widespread. It was a peculiarity of the bomber campaign that airmen often cycled to their aero-

Lancaster R5509 'EM–G' of 207 Squadron, Summer 1942. Note the differing camouflage denoting a replacement tail section; this aircraft failed to return from a mining sortie off Kiel Bay in August 1942, its seven crew all being listed on the Runnymede Memorial. (M. Claridge)

dromes after lunch, exchanging their wives, homes and normality for a few hours' war. Like the villagers, wives would listen for the rumble of the returning aircraft in the early hours. To them the biggest dread was a knock at the door.

Bad weather characterized the end of August, with the result that the number of last minute 'scrubs' began to rise again. However, local training could continue, and it was on one such flight that 207 Squadron suffered what were to be its last casualties at the unpopular aerodrome. In the early hours of August 19th, Flight Sergeant Fordwych was practising three engined overshoots when his Lancaster stalled at low level and hit the ground on the edge of Normanton, just beyond the threshold of the main runway. Wreckage littered the main road of the hamlet, and although there were miraculously no civilian casualties, all six crewmen were killed outright. Fordwych, aged 21, had come from Singapore to join the RAF, and he and his Australian engineer, John Murphy, were buried in the expanding Squadron plot at St. Mary's.

By now it was obvious that the situation with regard to resurfacing and repairs could not continue. On August 15th six aircraft had operated from

F/Lt 'Pat' Pattinson's Lancaster 'B–Beer' (R5908) on disperal at Syerston, September 1942. The 'dragon' nose art is probably inspired by the winged lion on 207 Squadron's crest. Pattinson flew a second tour with 207 later in the war: R5908 was shot down just over a month later. (M. Claridge)

Swinderby because the only runway into the wind was unserviceable. On the 23rd the Squadron's aircraft were officially detached to Syerston, whilst the conversion flight were sent to Swinderby. When by mid September there was still little progress with the runway repairs, Wing Commander Jeffs and Group Captain Swain decided that building work at Langar should be pushed ahead so that 207 could take up residence there as soon as possible. They arrived on the 20th, having flown 17 operations whilst at Syerston with a loss of four crews, and flew their first operation from Langar on the 23rd.

CHAPTER EIGHT

'Advance Australia!'

Bottesford did not reopen to flying until November 1942 when it became home to two squadrons. The first, 90 Squadron, had originally been formed for home defence in the Great War to counter the Zeppelin threat, and now found itself reactivated in 3 Group to fly Short's four engined heavy bomber, the Stirling. 90 was only a temporary lodger, and would return to 3 Group territory in East Anglia once ready for operations. Wing Commander John Claydon DFC became 90's new CO, but much of the work in reforming the squadron fell to the newly appointed adjutant, George Rawley, who in turn relied upon the experience of his NCO in charge of discipline, George Gee from Nottingham. The formation of a new unit was often used as a means of unloading unwanted personnel, so George Rawley insisted on interviewing every new posting, guided by George Gee:

Flight Sergeant Gee served with me at 3 Group H.Q., and in fact smoothed my path from civilian to useful member of the RAF. My time at Bottesford was more than occupied by the bumph associated with the work of forming the squadron. I billeted myself out with the Bottesford village butcher and his wife in the High Street. They were a benign old couple who looked after me very well. When we could snatch a few hours off Johnny Claydon used to take one or two of us to the Ram Jam Inn off the A1, or to Nottingham for the 'Hole in the Wall' or some other pub.

The first four Stirlings were delivered by pilots of the Air Transport Auxiliary between November 16–17th. Amongst the ferry pilots was Jim Mollinson, husband of the famous pre-war flier Amy Johnson, who was herself killed delivering an aircraft the previous year. Aircrews had also begun arriving, and within two weeks the Squadron was able to put up eight aircraft on a 'Bullseye', a night time cross-country exercise to accustom the crews to the demands of operational flying. To have the Squadron nearing readiness in just over a month was a remarkable achievement, especially considering that by now the aerodrome was also being shared with 467 Squadron Royal Australian Air Force. Cliff Allen, an engine fitter recently posted to 467, wrote:

It was several days before things got organized so a group of us went for a look around, doffed of course in gum boots. Our interest had been drawn by several Stirlings on the airfield, a type which most of us hadn't seen before. They were an awesome sight, so high up from the ground, and peering up under the undercarriage was like looking at a bridge superstructure.

For all its impressiveness, the Stirling's undercarriage was one of the design's weaknesses. On the morning of December 18th 90 Squadron's Flight Sergeant McGavin was informed that an undercarriage leg had buckled on one of the aircraft. He rushed down to the Flights and improvised a lashing with pieces of wood, but whilst underneath there was an audible groan and the unit collapsed completely, pinning him to the ground. The Squadron still had little equipment and by the time heavy lifting gear arrived from Norton Disney he was beyond help. Losses through operations were a sad but accepted reality, whereas deaths caused by faulty or poorly designed equipment were another matter entirely, and McGavin's loss caused some disquiet. With the endless fatigues, the incessant rain and the mud, morale sank lower still when rumours spread that all leave had been cancelled for Christmas. Wing Commander Claydon was so concerned that he had the Squadron paraded in No.2 hangar, where he explained that 48 Hour passes would be issued for those living within a 20 mile radius, and for the rest there would be the usual entertainment. He also announced their imminent departure to Ridgwell in Essex to commence operations. After two days stand-down for the usual festivities the advance party set out early on the morning of December 27th, the ground personnel entraining the next day at Bottesford station for their new home.

As already mentioned, during its last few weeks at Bottesford 90 Squadron had shared the station with 467 Squadron Royal Australian Air Force, which had been formed at Scampton on November 7th 1942 to fly Lancasters in 5 Group. 467 was Bomber Command's second Australian Lancaster squadron, the first being 1 Group's Binbrook-based 460 Squadron. These units had been formed in response to the wishes of the Australian government that Australian flying personnel should be grouped together wherever possible. Australians and New Zealanders accounted for roughly a tenth of bomber aircrew, but continuing losses meant that even nominally Australian squadrons could at best only hope to have 75% Australian crewmen. In the beginning Aussies were actually very sparse on 467, the majority of crewmen being English, Canadian or 'Kiwis'. Likewise the groundcrews were also predominantly RAF, and the handful of Australian NCOs on strength were mostly older reservists with little enthusiasm. Aubrey Tongue, a former Aircraftman armourer from Nottingham recalled visiting the Station Armoury to obtain a replacement turret cupola, the large perspex 'bubble' which covered the air gunner. Inside the armoury was a solitary Australian Flight Sergeant '...aged about ninety', sat on an ammunition box reading the *Daily Mirror*. Having taken his eyes off the newspaper long enough to ask Aubrey what he wanted, he wearily got to his feet and retrieved a battered Players tin from his pocket, prising the lid off at the same time to reveal various nuts and bolts inside. 'Here Son' he said handing over the tin, picking up the newspaper and resuming his seat, 'See if you can find one in there'!

At the age of 29, 467's commanding officer Wing Commander Cosme Gomm was a veteran. Tall and softly spoken, he was Brazilian born, but like the offspring of many expatriate families educated in England. He took up a

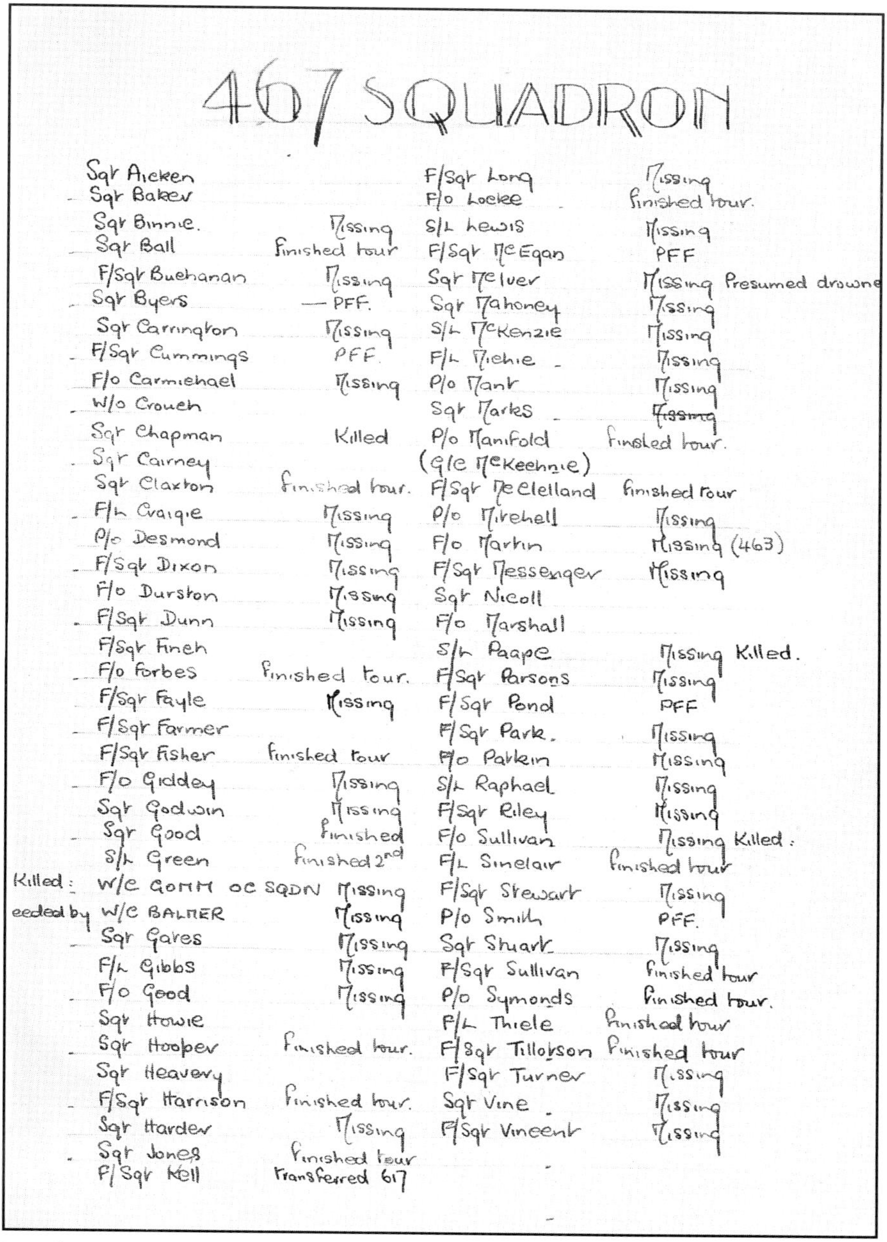

467 SQUADRON

Sgt Aicken	
Sgt Baker	
Sgt Binnie.	Missing
Sgt Ball	Finished tour
F/Sgt Buchanan	Missing
Sgt Byers	— PFF.
Sgt Carrington	Missing
F/Sgt Cummings	PFF.
F/O Carmichael	Missing
W/O Crouch	
Sgt Chapman	Killed
Sgt Cairney	
Sgt Claxton	Finished tour.
F/L Craigie	Missing
P/O Desmond	Missing
F/Sgt Dixon	Missing
F/O Durston	Missing
F/Sgt Dunn	Missing
F/Sgt Finch	
F/O Forbes	Finished tour.
F/Sgt Fayle	Missing
F/Sgt Farmer	
F/Sgt Fisher	Finished tour
F/O Giddey	Missing
Sgt Godwin	Missing
Sgt Good	Finished
S/L Green	Finished 2nd
Killed: W/C GOMM OC SQDN	Missing
eeded by W/C BALMER	Missing
Sgt Gates	Missing
F/L Gibbs	Missing
F/O Good	Missing
Sgt Howie	
Sgt Hooper	Finished tour.
Sgt Heavery	
F/Sgt Harrison	Finished tour.
Sgt Harder	Missing
Sgt Jones	Finished tour
F/Sgt Kell	Transferred 617

F/Sgt Long	Missing
F/O Locke	Finished tour.
S/L Lewis	Missing
F/Sgt McEgan	PFF
Sgt McIver	Missing Presumed drowne
Sgt Mahoney	Missing
S/L McKenzie	Missing
F/L Michie	Missing
P/O Mant	Missing
Sgt Marks	~~Missing~~
P/O Manifold	Finished tour.
(G/C McKechnie)	
F/Sgt McClelland	Finished tour
P/O Mitchell	Missing
F/O Martin	Missing (463)
F/Sgt Messenger	Missing
Sgt Nicoll	
F/O Marshall	
S/L Paape	Missing Killed.
F/Sgt Parsons	Missing
F/Sgt Pond	PFF
F/Sgt Park.	Missing
F/O Parkin	Missing
S/L Raphael	Missing
F/Sgt Riley	Missing
F/O Sullivan	Missing Killed.
F/L Sinclair	Finished tour
F/Sgt Stewart	Missing
P/O Smith	PFF.
Sgt Stuart	Missing
F/Sgt Sullivan	Finished tour
P/O Symonds	Finished tour.
F/L Thiele	Finished tour
F/Sgt Tillotson	Finished tour
F/Sgt Turner	Missing
Sgt Vine	Missing
F/Sgt Vincent	Missing

Page from the scrapbook of S/O Marie Cooper listing (most of) the captains on 467 Squadron, 1943. (M. Claridge) short service commission in the RAF on his 21st birthday, and by the outbreak of war was a Flight Lieutenant, completing his first tour on 77 Squadron, flying Whitleys. In April 1941 he was awarded a DFC and posted to 604 Squadron at Middle Wallop, a nightfighter unit operating Beaufighters under the famous 'Cat's Eyes' Cunningham. Whilst with 604 Gomm accounted for two Heinkels and a Junkers 88 before taking up a staff appointment prior to promotion to Wing Commander in June and his posting to 467 Squadron in November. He proved to be an excellent choice as CO of the new Australian squadron. He led by example, a quality which especially endeared him to the Aussies. Despite his quiet nature his eccentricities manifested themselves in the form of a huge two-seater Oldsmobile, widely envied in times of such strict petrol rationing, and his habit of toasting drinking companions with the words 'Never a Dull!'.

By a quirk of fate the Squadron's two flight commanders were both ex-207 Squadron Manchester pilots. 'B' Flight's Squadron Leader 'Pappy' Paape, a New Zealander in the RAF, had flown his tour from Waddington, but for Dave Green of 'A' Flight this was his second tour at Bottesford, and he arranged for his first tour navigator Warrant Officer 'Goldie' Goldstraw to join him.

Four crews were posted to the Squadron on the day that it was formed, to be joined by 16 more over the following three weeks. In terms of experience they were a mixed bunch. Most were fresh from OTU and were still waiting to be converted onto the Lancaster at 1661 Conversion Unit. Some were starting their second tours. Amongst the latter was 22-year-old Flight Lieutenant Keith Thiele RNZAF, who had reverted to Flight Lieutenant in order to return immediately to operations rather than become an instructor. A handful of crews had been posted from other squadrons mid-way through their tours. Tactics were constantly being evolved in the bomber war and most of these men resented their move, fearing that the enforced rest whilst 467 worked-up might adversely affect their chances of survival. The first six Lancasters landed at Bottesford on November 24th to be followed a few hours later by a truck convoy carrying the ground crews. True to form, Bottesford made an immediate impression. Flying surreptitiously in the mid-upper turret of one of the Lancasters was Alan Dickens, an engine fitter who had not fancied the uncomfortable truck ride and had secured a lift for himself, his bicycle and his kitbags. He recalled that the RCAF pilot of his Lancaster, Sergeant Al Wark (an American from Seattle) rapidly lost patience as he circled overhead, vainly peering through the gloom to find some landmark and begin his approach. In the end he called up Flying Control and demanded 'Where's the goddam airfield?'. He received two Very cartridges in reply.

December 1942, alternately icy and drizzly, was spent familiarising air and ground crews with their aircraft. It was not without risk, and the Squadron's first casualty came just three days before Christmas when Flying Officer Doug Bannerman RNZAF failed to return from a trip with a 207 Squadron crew from Langar. His crew were sent back to OTU to find another pilot, with the exception of his flight engineer who was assigned to Wing Commander Gomm.

The Squadron's first appearance on the 5 Group Order of Battle on January 2nd 1943 saw five crews detailed to take part in a mining sortie off France's Biscay ports. It was already dark as the Australian Sergeant Max Stewart's 'J-Jig' reached the end of runway 21 and his bomb aimer flashed the identity letter to the chequered control van. On receiving an answering 'green' Stewart advanced the throttles, being careful to give a little more power to the port engines and a touch of right rudder to counteract the usual swing on take-off. Heavily laden, she was slow to gain momentum, but soon the white runway lights were flashing beneath, and as her tail lifted and windows rattled with the rising note of her engines, 'Jig' slowly clawed into the air. To the small group who had gathered to wave the aircraft off she was visible as a steady pair of red and green lights as she laboured low over Beacon Hill in the direction of the red glow marking the spire of St. Mary's. In the hours between the fading rumble of the last bomber and the crackling voice over the R/T announcing their return, tension was high, particularly amongst the groundcrews who had prepared the aircraft. But all returned safely, although Sergeant Stewart diverted to Predannack in Cornwall after what was described as 'A pleasant and rather successful trip'.

Following another gardening sortie, five crews took part in a small scale trial run for Pathfinder Force Mosquitoes, testing the new 'Oboe' blind bombing device for dropping target markers. The target was Essen, and two aircraft were forced to return early due to compass and rear turret failure respectively. Of the others Flight Lieutenant Keith Thiele's Lancaster was hit by flak over the target, holing both wings and damaging a propeller blade, and Jim Michie's bomb aimer passed out through lack of oxygen, forcing him to release the bombs himself. The following night's raid on Duisberg was particularly disappointing. Although five aircraft were detailed, a spate of last minute problems meant that only Sergeants Stewart and Wark were able to get away. Stewart returned safely, but Al Wark and his crew did not return and are commemorated on the Runnymede Memorial[1].

[1] He was not the only American to be killed on the Squadron. Bill Komaiko, navigator on Jim Michie's crew who were lost on February 19th was from Chicago, Illinois.

CHAPTER NINE

The Big City

Bad weather was the norm at Bottesford even when other aerodromes in the locality were clear, but for several days in January 1943 all 1 and 5 Group airfields were closed in by thick, impenetrable fog. There was little to do on camp on miserable days such as these, so the attractions of Nottingham, Grantham or Newark particularly beckoned. Cliff Allen wrote:

If weekend passes were issued my mate Maxie Byrne and I always headed for Nottingham, where drinking was the main pastime. We had our meals at the Y.M.C.A., and the last train back was round about 11.30, which we always missed, so that meant finding somewhere to sleep. Nottingham was crowded with thousands of servicemen, and the last hope, the Salvation Army hostel was always booked up. You wouldn't believe the places we slept or tried to sleep, the Police Station, the General Hospital, empty railway carriages, even a telephone box. This was very cold in winter, and a bit cramped for two!

In order to break the monotony for his crew, Flight Sergeant Brian Howie RAAF, skipper of 'A-Apple' suggested a trip to Nottingham. Fellow Australian Ted Done, his wireless operator, takes up the story:

We booked into our usual boarding house, and then off to the well-stocked bar in the Palais de Danse and the girls. The time came to return to the house, sleep it off, catch a bus and get back to the station, but no buses were running until much too late for us, and instead army ammunition trucks gave us a lift back. On arrival we were met with the news that we were supposed to be in briefing. The others hurried on, but nature dictated that I do otherwise before rushing down to SHQ, only to be confronted by an armed sentry outside the building who demanded identification before allowing me through. To my amazement there were two more inside. Never before had this happened. Hurrying forward I ran into the Station Commander as he came out of his office. He stopped me in my tracks with a 'Who the Hell are you?'. On identifying myself and my reasons for being there he told the sentry to take my name and number and to let him have it after briefing. Turning to me he said, 'You should be charged with causing another to fly in your place. I'll see you later'. On entering the room I momentarily became the centre of attention, but all eyes, including mine, went back to the huge wall map showing the target. The unusual presence of the sentries was explained, for Berlin was to have our attention that night.

This marked the first attack on Berlin since the débâcle in November 1941, hence the elaborate security. The clear conditions rendered the mark-

F/Sgt Brian Howie RAAF sits in the cockpit of his usual aircraft, 'A-Apple' ED541. Already operational on 50 Squadron, it was hoped that the macabre artwork would bring the crew good luck on their posting to 467: they completed their tour on 9th March 1943 — the first to do so. (T.E. Done)

ing flares easily visible, but at the altitude the bombers were flying temperatures were extremely low, around minus fifty degrees centigrade, and as a consequence Keith Thiele flying 'D-Dog', again found himself in trouble. On the run-in to the target his Canadian rear gunner, 21-year-old Alvin Broemeling, reported that his oxygen apparatus was freezing up. A few days before, Broemeling had found that his flying helmet had been stolen from the locker room. He was issued with a replacement by the Station Clothing Store but soon after take-off on the 16th told Thiele that his new helmet was uncomfortably tight. Thiele advised him to switch to the spare always carried on board, but unfortunately this helmet had an obsolete oxygen mask lacking the inspiratory valve fitted to newer models to prevent freezing. Whilst aircrew were constantly wary of the risk of frostbite brought about by contact between unprotected skin and metal, anoxia was far more dangerous because the victim was often unaware of it. The build-up of ice in the oxygen tube slowly starved the brain of air, leading to unconsciousness and death. Mindful of this, Thiele told Broemeling to use the emergency bottles, which initially seemed to help, but by the time they began their bomb run at 19,000 feet Broemeling was again experiencing problems. The wireless operator was despatched aft to help as best he could whilst Thiele concentrated on completing the run, and the second that bombs were released, ignoring the fact that they were still over Berlin's heavy flak defences, Thiele put the Lancaster into a steep dive. He continued to lose height until at 8,000 feet they were below the oxygen level. He then put the aircraft on autopilot and went back himself, leaving the flight engineer to keep an eye on the controls. The unconscious Broemeling had fallen against the turret doors, and with some difficulty Thiele managed to get himself half inside and lever him out. Whilst he was doing this the aircraft was buffeted by flak bursts and was actually hit twice. Having placed Broemeling on the rest bed, Thiele regained control and they limped back to Bottesford, but despite the best efforts of the crew to revive him the unfortunate gunner did not regain consciousness and when Doc Howarth, the Squadron M.O., met them at their dispersal with the ambulance, he declared that Broemeling had been dead for several hours. He was subsequently buried in St. Swithun's churchyard, Long Bennington, the first to be interred in the special squadron plot and perhaps the most tragic because he was more a victim of petty theft than of war.

After such an eventful night there were loud mutterings on the following day when briefing revealed that Berlin was again the target. Ted Done wrote:

As A-for-Apple taxied into position for take-off each one of us experienced churning stomachs and nervous tension, hiding his feelings as best he could. We were on our way. Mac (nav) gave Brian the course for the first leg and we settled down to our various jobs. Suddenly Brian discovered that his compass was 180 degrees opposed to the other and that we were heading for Ireland and had been doing so for seven minutes. We immediately swung around and flew back, crossing our 'drome fifteen minutes behind the others. Normally we should not have continued, but being keyed

W/Cdr Gomm and crew wait for take-off, March 1943. In the meantime they drink tea provided by the NAAFI waggon. Left to right: F/O Roy Hare, S/Ldr Evans (of the 5 Group Navigation staff), W/Cdr Gomm, Sgt James Lee and Sgt A. Brown. (M. Palmer)

Aircrews gather outside the 'B' Flight office to await transport to take them to their aircraft, March 1943. Note the pigeons in their containers on the pathway, intended as an aid to air-sea rescue, and the varied flying gear. (G.E. Fitt)

up this standing instruction was ignored and Mac came up with a new course. Just before reaching Bornholm he said 'We're still fifteen minutes behind, the head wind must be a lot stronger than Met. gave us'. Not liking the idea of being the last over the target and thus being prey for all the enraged nightfighters, we again decided to go against instructions and cut the corner, entering Berlin from the NW instead of the NE.

The sky was crystal clear, the stars winking, and as usual Brian was losing and then gaining altitude, swinging from side to side to lessen the chances of interception but always steadily approaching the target area. Suddenly, several searchlights sprang into being, waving backwards and forwards looking for the intruder. Seconds later a brilliant blue-green light snapped directly on to us, to be immediately followed by the others. Now the flak started. The glare was intense and blinding, and from the ground it must have appeared that we were impaled on the apex of those shafts of light. Shells were bursting all around, those below lifting us with sledgehammer like blows, those beside would buffet us sideways, sometimes lifting the wing on that side with violent thrusts. By this time we had lost height and were down to 8,000 feet, nearly in reach of the lethal light flak which was now coming up at us in streams of coloured balls. For the whole of this time, standing in the astrodome and clinging to the supports, I was trying my hardest to out-guess the gunners below and issuing direction after direction to Brian, when, as with a single

Fifty years on — the derelict 'B' Flight office today. The door and pathway remain, albeit overgrown. The chimney for the pot-bellied stove has gone, but in the extreme distance the stumps on the landing ground have grown into trees. (W.R. Baguley)

switch all the lights went out, the flak momentarily ceased, and we were through. Only as we straightened up did searchlights spring into being in front of us and to the north east. The others had arrived... At debriefing we found that all the others had been late over the target because of that stronger headwind, whilst we had both increased speed and cut corners so as not to be the lone aircraft over the city! A lesson learned. This was my 27th trip, only three to go.

At the beginning of March, after over a year as Station Commander, Group Captain Swain handed over to Group Captain W.N. McKechnie GC, but before he left the Australians managed to incur 'Ferdie's' displeasure in a dramatic way. Keith Thiele recalled:

I well remember the time we had a visit from some high dignitary organised by Swain. I think from memory it was a duchess, and for weeks all was spit and polish to prepare for her visit, with borders to paths whitewashed, etc. and the Officers' Mess made immaculate. I vaguely remember the very irate Groupie arriving at the Mess at about midnight on the night before her visit to find a roaring party in progress. There were foot and bum prints on the ceiling, with the rooms covered in a generous layer of ash from the various flares that had been ignited. I don't recall whether it was on that occasion or on another that the piano had also suffered somewhat after some irresponsible Kiwi had performed a Maori Harka on the strings...

An old Cranwellian and a contemporary of Douglas Bader, Group Captain William McKechnie bore the distinction of being the only cadet ever to win the George Cross whilst under training. In October 1929 whilst on circuits and bumps he witnessed a fellow cadet crash his biplane and slump unconscious as it burst into flames. He immediately landed beside the unfortunate man and dragged him to safety, being badly burned in the process. In character McKechnie was a complete opposite to Swain, and could often be seen at the end of the runway waving to the crews as they took off on 'ops'. Some aircrew would acknowledge him with a cheerful 'V' sign as they sped past, to which he would proffer a wide grin and a rigid salute. Section Officer Marie Cooper also took part in this nightly ritual, and in response to complaints that she couldn't be seen, took to wearing a pair of brightly coloured Norwegian ski gloves for identification. On entering Flying Control one evening following take-off she was confronted by a throng of visiting high ranking officers accompanied by McKechnie. Not until she had given them her smartest salute did she realise that she was still wearing her gloves, and although they were a patriotic red, white and blue, they were hardly a regulation item of dress. Fortunately McKechnie was very understanding, although in future he forbade her to come anywhere near high ranking visitors!

The aerodrome received an even more unusual group of visitors one wet blustery day in March. The Lancasters were lining up at the end of the runway when a fox came streaking across the airfield hotly pursued by the Belvoir hunt. The riders, resplendent in scarlet coats and blowing horns for all they were worth looked neither to the left nor to the right as they galloped across the runway. Flying Control was far from amused and there was much swearing over the R/T from the bemused captains nursing overheating engines. The event demonstrated more than any other that even the war could not change some things.

In other ways too March was eventful. A handful of crews were drawn from 'A' and 'B' Flights to form 'C' Flight, and placed under the command of the newly promoted (again) Squadron Leader Thiele. As regards operations, there were targets such as Berlin (three times), Essen (twice), Hamburg, Nuremburg, Munich, Stuttgart and Duisberg. On the 22nd it was St. Nazaire in France. Weather was clear over the target area with bright moonlight, good visibility and only a slight ground haze. Large fires were reported in the dock area, and the defences were gradually overwhelmed as the attack progressed. However, on return the Midlands were swathed in a thick band of cloud so the crews were instructed to divert to Lossiemouth in Scotland. Pilot Officer Stewart Hooper RAAF, on this occasion flying ED500 PO-S wrote:

Diverted to Lossiemouth, mine was the first to land. My story is that they landed me down wind, and I ran off the end of the strip, hit a hole and pushed the tail wheel into the fuselage, hardly a prang at all. The kites following were diverted to Kinloss

W/Cdr Gomm talks to G/Capt Swain whilst the crew of P/O G.S. Mant RAAF are given their post-raid debriefing by an Intelligence Officer. The Mant crew were shot down on the night of 11/12th March 1943 after attacking Stuttgart. (M. Claridge)

about ten or twenty miles away, but nothing was said, there was no enquiry and no queries.'

As it was, there had been enough enquiries for one month. When one Pilot Officer 'Dinny' Mant (known as 'Trailing Aerial' because of his lankiness) and crew failed to return from Stuttgart, it was the responsibility of the Committee of Adjustment to process their personal effects. Corporal Ron Shaw from Nottingham recalled:

After quite a spell in the Central Registry I became NCO i/c the Committee of Adjustment. Along with four WAAF helpers we dealt with the service and personal effects of missing and deceased aircrew and airmen. There was always a considerable amount of paperwork involved, the personal effects being sent eventually to a central depository at Colnbrook near Slough, where they could be claimed by the next of kin. The Committee of Adjustment office was in a large Nissen hut not far from SHQ marked 'Out of Bounds to all Ranks'. I was responsible to Squadron Leader Cedric Gibbs in the SHQ, and one morning he phoned me to go and see a young woman in the Guard Room. She was hoping to recover something she had bought for a missing airman, and mentioned in passing that she was engaged to him. Unfortunately I couldn't help, but two days later Gibbs phoned again. There was another woman in the Guard Room — engaged to the same man! I later got into trouble for

Twenty-four year old F/Lt Jack Sullivan (left) from Queensland talks to F/Sgt 'Freddie' Wilmot following their return from a raid, Spring 1943. Wilmot and his crew failed to return from Dusseldorf in June, whilst the Sullivan crew were lost whilst attacking Milan in August. (M. Claridge)

destroying mail belonging to him. As far as I was concerned there was already enough heartache, so it was better to lose them. It was about this time that the Squadron Adjutant was dismissed from the RAF and sentenced to six months in Lincoln prison for stealing missing aircrew effects.

It transpired that the Adjutant had been helping himself to particularly choice items. With a rising percentage of the missing being Australian, there was little chance of their families querying any irregularities. However, a member of Dinny Mant's crew on commissioning leave returned to discover his friends missing and his belongings erroneously removed from the hut he shared with them. On reporting the mistake everything was quickly returned to him with the exception of a wireless set, of which no record could be found. Accusations followed, and a search of the Adjutant's rented house in Bottesford village not only revealed the missing radio, but a large quantity of other items. With such damning evidence the court martial was merely a formality, and a few days after sentencing the whole Squadron was paraded between the hangars. The unfortunate officer was marched before them, and with drums rolling, the rank lace was torn from his sleeves and he was led away in tears.

CHAPTER TEN

Happy Valley

By early 1943 the Commander-in-Chief of Bomber Command, Air Chief Marshall Sir Arthur Harris, believed that it was now ready for a sustained assault on Germany, the first stage of which began in April with the so-called 'Battle of the Ruhr'. The campaign lasted for four months with the majority of raids concentrated on cities in the Ruhr Valley. Berlin aside, the Ruhr had the most formidable defences in Europe, and as 1943 continued losses steadily began to increase. Between April and July alone fifteen crews failed to return to Bottesford. Life in the air was all too frequently short and brutal, the squalid conditions on temporary aerodromes offering little comfort. In this sense Bottesford was worse than most. Mud and damp apart, the station had a population twice that of any of the surrounding villages. With its Post Office, church, cinema, barbers, tailors and grocery shop it offered most of the facilities of a village, but on the minus side its 2,000 inhabitants were crowded into prefabricated huts with neither adequate heating nor sanitation. True, the nearby villages were no better provided for and, unlike the aerodrome, did not even have the benefits of electricity or running water. In Bottesford mains water was not supplied until 1951, sewers coming ten years later. Until then the eleven hundred villagers made do with wells, hand pumps and earth closets. The RAF tended to attract those with technical backgrounds, frequently from large cities, and rural life was a revelation to them. LACW Doris George who worked in the Equipment Section recalled:

My friend Muriel Carpenter and I used to go to the dances at Long Bennington and had our dancing polished up for us by the station barber, Phil Dresman, and by the station cobbler. We also used to visit the pubs opposite the village hall, mainly the Wheatsheaf and the Reindeer. The Black Boy at Foston was also very popular, but the Wheatsheaf was of particular note because it was without mod cons still and had wooden twin seating in the toilets!

Back on the station, unless one was an officer and had a batman to provide it, hot water for morning ablutions was an extremely rare commodity. The Airmens' Mess provided buckets on request, but the prospect of walking half a mile from the billets for a wash and possibly joining the breakfast queue as the shutters were pulled down appealed to few. Group Captain McKechnie — tired of the endless complaints — declared, 'If I can shave in cold water - so can you!'. Nevertheless, there was also humour in the degradations. Arthur Cackett, a fitter IIE remembered:

Bottesford was a very primitive station for hygiene. On the communal site there were no flush toilets, just pans which had to be emptied, and so many of the Ground Staff General Duties were paid 3d per day extra to go around with a lorry and collect the pans for emptying in heaps over the surrounding fields. There was a terrible smell if the wind was blowing in your direction! It was rather a crude joke amongst the lads who moved it, who chalked on the side of their lorry: 'You shoot it — we'll shift it!'.

There was also a serious side to the situation in that the insanitary conditions could all too easily provide a breeding ground for epidemics. To counter such a threat there were periodic medical inspections, known as the F.F.I.s, or 'Free from Infection'. One such inspection in early April 1943 revealed a case of diphtheria and led to the aerodrome being sealed off for ten days. Cliff Allen wrote:

It was very late one night, all in our Nissen hut were sound asleep when the door burst open and a voice bellowed 'Wakey, Wakey!'. It was totally dark but we found out the interlopers were the Medical Officer, a medical orderly and the duty Sergeant. The M.O. said, 'A case of diphtheria has been found on the station and I'm here with my assistant to inspect you all. You don't have to get out of bed, just throw back your blanket and lower your pyjamas'. He approached the first bed and shone a torch at the head and neck of the occupant who was half asleep. Then he moved to the lower parts, and whilst he shone the light his assistant poked around with a pencil. Everyone in the hut was checked, and as they were leaving someone shouted, 'Did you find it?'.

Arthur Cackett had less to laugh about:

Everyone had to report to sick quarters for inoculations. Quite a few WAAFs and airmen went down with diphtheria after this, and I was one of them. I was rushed forty miles away to an isolation hospital in Leicester (Groby Road) where I spent six weeks on my back and lost a stone and a half in weight. After I returned to Bottesford I was in and out of sick bay for months before I got really well again, but I've never regained the weight I lost. I still have my pay book, and in it are three entries in red ink stating that I refused further inoculations.

For some others the situation had unexpected bonuses. Sergeant Harold Hernaman, wireless operator on Pilot Officer Bill Manifold's crew remembered:

Being given some leave I decided not to go home for a change, so I collected a rail warrant for Bude in Cornwall. After a long rail journey I arrived, disliked what I saw, so paid my hotel bill and returned to Nottingham. By then I was very short of cash, so I went to the Palais expecting to see some off-duty Squadron members from whom I could borrow a few shillings. However, there was no-one there. By now, with insufficient funds to buy a rail ticket I set out to walk and hitch-hike. On arrival at the Guard Room in the early hours of the morning I was informed that once inside the camp I would be quarantined. The whole camp was in isolation, except, I may add, for aircrew on operations. Interesting speculation, if one of us had been shot down and taken prisoner, subsequently infecting the Germans, would we have been guilty of practising germ warfare? Anyway, during the quarantine period I played endless poker, and by the time my leave had expired had amassed a total of some £80.

By the end of the scare one WAAF had died and several others were seriously ill. During the quarantine, eighteen WAAF cooks had to be isolated, confined to their quarters. The remainder in the cookhouse were therefore forced to work 24 hour shifts until the crisis was over, for which they were highly commended by 5 Group headquarters. But as Harold Hernaman pointed out, operations continued throughout the crisis. To avoid any contravention of the Geneva Convention the crews were advised by the M.O. that if shot down and captured they should inform the Germans immediately of the possibility of their being a carrier. However, the general consensus was that this might lead to an immediate cure by way of a bullet, so it was decided to say nothing.

On April 3rd crews were briefed for an attack on the infamous Krupps works in Essen, marking the start of the Squadron's contribution to the Battle of the Ruhr. Although producing a better concentration of bombs on this target than ever before, 'B' Flight's Squadron Leader Paape and crew were shot down on the Dutch-German border. Paape always insisted that his Lancaster be referred to as 'T-Thomas' rather than the more familiar 'T-Tommy'. He also assured the numerous sceptics in the Mess that his own method for a successful run-in to the target was to engage 'George' the auto-pilot and to close his eyes... After this raid it was decided that Dave Green of 'A' Flight had done enough and he was rested from operations, being officially posted 'Tour Expired' in June. In the meantime his experience was needed elsewhere, and in May he was seconded to the US Eighth Air Force's 44th Bomber Group at Shipdham in Norfolk as an advisor. The Americans were interested in the feasibility of night operations, and during May USAAF B-24 Liberators were frequent visitors to Bottesford, with Wingco Gomm taking the 44th's Lieutenant Dickson to Duisberg on the 12th May.

In mid April the Squadron took part in the first raid on the Italian naval base at La Spezia. Opposition over Italian targets was often far less than over Germany, a fact emphasised by the derisive painting of ice cream cones rather than bombs on the aircraft to denote such missions. On the minus side, the long flight over the Alps was extremely tiring, sometimes lasting ten or eleven hours. In the shortening spring nights this meant that a good proportion of the journey had to be made in daylight, increasing the chances of interception. Also hazardous were the notorious electrical storms encountered over the Alps and southern France. Another long distance raid on April 16/17th on the Skoda armaments factory at Pilsen in Czechoslovakia met with disastrous results. Markers and the majority of bombs fell around a

The morning after ..... All too obvious Flak damage to the starboard outer engine of Lancaster LM310 following S/Ldr Keith Thiele's crash-landing at Coltishall in the early hours of 13th May 1943. (K.F. Thiele)

mental asylum seven miles from the factory. As well as the large loss of life on the ground, two of the fifteen 467 crews taking part failed to return. When on the 18th the Squadron was stood down, this was therefore taken as a general opportunity to put aside woes in the Mess bar. Unfortunately Group had other ideas, and as the afternoon wore on orders were received for another attack on Spezia. It required a gargantuan effort by the groundcrews to ready the aircraft, but Vern Howarth was far from happy. He told Wing Commander Gomm in no uncertain terms that 'well oiled' as they were, he considered the aircrew unfit to fly. A heated discussion followed, and Gomm and Howarth were still arguing beside the runway as the Lancasters took off. Howarth's worries proved unfounded, and perhaps there was even a lesson to be learned, for almost all of the crews brought back photographs showing the target area...

Despite a spell of bad weather at the start of May there were three further raids on Ruhr targets, with Flight Lieutenant Craigie failing to return from Essen on the 1st. On the 12th Keith Thiele limped back from Duisberg on two engines after a direct hit from flak on his bombing run severed the rear half of the starboard outer, punctured the starboard inner and blew out most of the perspex in the cockpit. In addition he was struck on the head by a shell

Celebrations for the award of Keith Thiele's DSO — the first on 467 Squadron. Raising a glass are, left to right: 'Jock' Murray (Mess landlord), Cosme Gomm, Keith Thiele, Group Captain McKechnie, Don MacKenzie and 'Ray' Raphael. Within a few months four of the six would be dead. (M. Claridge)

splinter. Since the starboard inner also drove one of the two pumps powering the hydraulic system he could not lower the undercarriage and was forced to 'belly in' at Coltishall from where he and his crew were collected the following day by Group Captain McKechnie. He recalls that McKechnie burst out laughing when he apologized for making 'such a crook landing'. Despite its seemingly terminal state Thiele's 'O-Orange' was soon on its way to the Lancaster repair organization, eventually returning to service with 106 Squadron. In the meantime Thiele's determination and skill were rewarded with an immediate award of the DSO, the first on the Squadron. When Thiele finished his tour at the start of June he again offered to revert to Flight Lieutenant to return to operations, but had to make do with a posting to Ferry Command[1].

Following a second fruitless attack on Pilsen, hampered by smoke haze, there were a few days respite during which 617 Squadron at Scampton carried out its legendary raid on the Ruhr dams. In a strange twist of fate their first casualty was Pilot Officer V.W. Byers RCAF, who just weeks before had begun his first tour with 467 at Bottesford. He and his crew completed just three operations before being chosen for the new squadron, disproving the myth that all the crews were highly experienced. Briefed to attack the Möhne

[1] His long standing ambition had been to be a fighter pilot and he was to end the war as CO of 3 Squadron, flying Tempests in the 2nd Tactical Air Force, having been awarded the DSO DFC**.

dam, his was the third aircraft off in the second wave. Having misidentified his landfall in the Frisians he gained height in an attempt to confirm his position, inadvertently coming within range of the notorious radar guided flak on the island of Texel. Only the body of the rear gunner was recovered, a testament to the folly of sending inexperienced crews on such demanding operations.

As a follow up to the Dams raid a 'maximum effort' was mounted on Dortmund, the 826 crews taking part making this the largest raid since the 'Thousand Force' attacks the previous summer. 467 managed to despatch a record 24 aircraft after a phenomenal effort from the ground crews. Perhaps the fact that it was 24th May, 'Empire Day' had spurred them on, and now that the Squadron was gaining an excellent reputation for itself, journalists were on hand to record the observations of the returning crews:

From a special correspondent. A Bomber Command Station, Monday.

Aircrews of a record-breaking Australian Lancaster squadron who took part in the raid told their stories today. Enthusiastic over the success of their station in the safe return to its base of each bomber, the pilots, observers and gunners unanimously described the raid as 'the best ever'.

The first bomb fell at one o'clock. Within an hour many hundreds of aircraft, the majority of them four engined, had unloaded over 2,000 tons of bombs, including dozens of 4,000 pounders. They caused huge fires in the industrial part of the city and smoke which billowed up to 20,000 feet.

In the first of the great waves of bombers was Wing Commander Cosme Gomm DFC, the Brazilian leader of this Australian squadron. This tall veteran of 51 raids was coned by searchlights on his bombing run, but flew on and dropped his bombs on the target. 'They turned everything on us,' he said, 'but we were struck only by a couple of splinters. I saw a German fighter shot down in flames over the Channel'.

Also on the raid, making his first trip in a Lancaster, was the commander of the station, Group Captain W.N. McKechnie. Pilot Officer Roy Hare said that all he saw were 'some gondolas going down the high street' — a sly reference to the devastating Ruhr floods caused by the shattering of the Mohne Dam last week. Great stretches of flood water north-west of the target were seen by Flight Lieutenant Raphael of Fulham, pilot of 'U for Uncle'. 'We guessed that the banks of the canal had overflowed' he said. A member of the crew of 'U for Uncle' which limped home on three engines summed up: 'I guess Dortmund isn't much use for anything else now.'

Despite his comments, Gomm had been fixed by searchlights for over six minutes, blinded by the glare and running the gauntlet of the flak as he concentrated on his run-in. Group Captain McKechnie received similar punishment for four and a half minutes. Station commanders were not supposed to fly on operations because they were far too valuable to lose, but despite suffering chronic air sickness McKechnie flew whenever he could find an excuse. However, because of his airsickness crews used any excuse *not* to fly with him! The Dortmund raid netted an unusually high proportion of aiming point photographs, and soon afterwards there was further cause

Two groundcrew proudly show their crude (in more ways than one) shelter on the dispersal used by W/O 'Pluto' Wilson's Lancaster, Bottesford, Summer 1943. (P.G. Barry)

for celebration when Sergeant Frank Heavery's crew became the first on the Squadron to complete a whole first tour at Bottesford. Eddie Foster, navigator on the crew wrote:

We could expect an immediate and much more relaxed nine days leave now we had finished, but before that the long promised party for the groundcrew had to be organized. Most of them had set out as sprogs with us and were a grand bunch of lads. They might play hell with us if we brought back a slightly battered Lancaster, but they would cheerfully work around the clock if it meant getting us back safely. As we adjourned to the village pub in Long Bennington, the seven of us got together a kitty to provide beer for the evening's festivities. But the erks had other ideas. They were giving us the send-off, and soon the pints provided were being augmented by their contributions of the hard stuff. The events are a little hazy now, in fact they were not too clear the following morning, but I do recall the landlord calling time, at which point a large Leading Aircraftman tripped me and leapt across my chest with a huge claspknife in his hand. Surely, I thought, this silly sod is not blaming me for all the ventilation holes in his hydraulics? I need not have worried, for he turned out to be souvenir hunter and I willingly settled for the loss of my stripes and 'flying arsehole' (The 'O' wing worn by Observers). *Which was why my family were surprised next day when their favourite flyer arrived home a rather dishevelled AC2. They should have been pleased, as I was, that he had not returned as a boy soprano...*

CHAPTER ELEVEN

Shuttle to Friedrichshaven

June 1943 began with thundery rain meaning a few days stand-down. The respite ended on the 11th when conditions improved enough for eighteen crews to be briefed for an attack on Dusseldorf. Squadron Leader Ambrose had arrived two days before to take over command of 'C' Flight, and found himself flying that night as second dickey with his 'B' Flight colleague, 'Mac' MacKenzie. Also with them was the Gunnery Leader, Bob Betts, on this, the 28th operation of MacKenzie's tour. The aircraft took off between 22.30 hours and midnight, the ORB commenting:

All the 467 aircraft took off in spite of heavy thunder showers and thick mist on the aerodrome, and it was a bleak sight as they splashed their way through the puddles down the runway.

The Lancasters began returning around 5 am the following morning, announcing their arrival to flying control and asking permission to 'pancake'. Congestion in the air meant that returning aircraft would be stacked in the circuit at 1,000 feet intervals, gradually descending as they waited for their turn to land. In charge of Flying Control at Bottesford was an officer by the unfortunate name of Squadron Leader Flowerdew. Unfortunate, that is, because the aerodrome's callsign was 'Flowerbed'. As a consequence, mischievous captains exhilarated to be back would often regale him over the R/T with 'Hallo Flowerdew, Hallo Flowerdew', to which his reply would be an emphatic 'Hallo..., Hallo..., this is FLOWERBED, this is FLOWERBED. Over'!

On the morning of the 12th, however, the mood in Flying Control was a sombre one. Of MacKenzie and Flight Sergeant Freddie Wilmot nothing more was heard. 467 had lost two flight commanders and a gunnery leader in one night, and in Mac MacKenzie a universally liked founding member of the Squadron. Marie Cooper recalled that the New Zealander's tousled blonde head was always a welcome sight at debriefing. Fond of the 'Inkspots', and the proud owner of an Opel sports car, Don MacKenzie was a few weeks short of his 22nd birthday. His successor on 'B' Flight was Keith Sinclair, a former journalist from Melbourne who had the distinction of being one of few foreign reporters to be granted an interview with Adolf Hitler before the war. He broke ground on 467 in that he was the Squadron's first Australian flight commander. On the same day that Keith Sinclair was appointed to fill MacKenzie's shoes it was officially announced that Wing Commander Gomm had been awarded the DSO for his leadership over the past few months. The award was a popular one and within a short time he was again to demonstrate his virtuosity, and in so doing, bring about two 'firsts' for the Command.

For some months 5 Group had been toying with the problem of hitting precision targets. Pathfinder marking had improved general accuracy, but a myriad of unpredictable such as changing winds, cloud, industrial haze or even enemy decoys were often encountered at the last minute leading to further errors. A growing body of opinion felt that these could be reduced by having an experienced captain actually orbiting the target area and calling out corrections to the rest of the force over the R/T. Such an approach had been quite successful on the recent Dams raid and in a daylight attack on the Schneider armaments factory at Le Creusot in October 1942, but never before had it been tested at night on a conventional target. Now Intelligence had discovered that the Zeppelin factory at Friedrichshaven on the shores of Lake Constance was being used for the production of Wurzburg ground radar sets,vital for the control of German nightfighters. As a single factory such a small target would offer an excellent opportunity to test the new procedure, and as a further departure the crews were instructed to fly south to recently captured airfields in North Africa. This was to be the first of what subsequently became known as the 'Shuttle Raids', and meant not only that the German nightfighters waiting over France could be outwitted, but that another target could be bombed with equal surprise on their eventual return.

Rumours first began to circulate at Bottesford when the Equipment Section took delivery of khaki shorts, bush shirts and a quantity of prewar pith helmets more in keeping with the North West frontier than a busy bomber station. Further fuel was added when the Squadron's most experienced crews spent a week practising 'radio controlled bombing' at Wainfleet range on the Wash. After weeks of preparation, on the evening of June 21st eight aircraft took off from Bottesford to join the 'Operation Bellicose' attack force led by Group Captain Slee. Having formed up off the coast of France they carried out a feint towards the Ruhr before dog-legging south. Unfortunately, in the process Slee's aircraft received a flak hit and he was forced to hand over to his deputy, Wing Commander Gomm. Violent electrical storms were encountered over France, and the aircraft were viciously buffeted by turbulence. Flashes of lightning lit the clouds from within and static electricity danced between gun barrels and propeller blades. However, as they prepared to make the final run-in to the target the clouds below them parted and Friedrichshaven could be clearly seen in the hazy moonlight. Gomm reported afterwards:

Sortie completed. Clear, moon not much effect due to high cloud. Took over at rendezvous point 0225. Flares dropped by P.F.F. 0238 to E of target. 0239 PFF red about 1 1/2 miles E of target. 0240 green T.I. 400 yards E of target. 0241 own a/c dropped green T.I. and flares dropped on target. 0243 a/c ordered to attack visually. 0244 P.F.F. offered to back up T.I. and permission granted. 0247 own a/c dropped green

The morning of 22nd June 1943. W/Cdr Gomm and his crew at Blida, Algeria following 'Operation Bellicose', the daring raid on the Zeppelin works at Friedrichshaven. (R. Hare)

T.I. 0247 indirect bombing ordered due to number of T.I.'s scattered about. 0302 attack completed. Bombed green T.I. nearest target, own bombing not observed, obscured by smoke. Other bombs seen to fall on SE corner of shed. The attack could have been successful but for the following reasons:

Illumination. Not effective owing to high cloud.
Not sufficient flares.
First green T.I. accurate but backers-up too far from target.
Heavier opposition than expected.
There was very little wind over target.
A controlled attack (Radio Telephone) can and will be successful.

The report made no mention of the fact that Gomm's dissatisfaction with the marking led him to make his own attempt at extremely low level, attracting the attention of all the light flak in the vicinity. Despite his pessimism, post-raid reconnaissance estimated that ten percent of the bombs struck the factory, causing serious damage. Although there were no losses, several aircraft sustained flak damage. Keith Sinclair's PO-Z had an engine almost severed over the target. With the help of his flight engineer, Paddy Traynor, he managed to extinguish the flames and nurse the Lancaster through al-

S/Ldr Keith Sinclair and his Flight Engineer Sgt Paddy Traynor in the cockpit of their usual aircraft 'Pregnant Winnie'.

pine valleys to the Mediterranean, Blida and safety. Spares would take several weeks to reach North Africa, so when on the 23rd the returning crews bombed La Spezia, Sinclair borrowed Stu Hooper's Lancaster. The latter, now tour expired, was in no hurry to go anywhere. When the seven crews landed back at Bottesford in the early hours of June 24th they brought with them ample supplies of grapes, wine and bananas, and enough cases of sunburn and the dreaded 'Gyppo Tummy' to keep SSQ busy for some time to come.

CHAPTER TWELVE

On the other side of the hill

July saw a continuing interest in Italian targets, and on the afternoon of the 12th eighteen crews were briefed for an attack on Turin. The route required the bombers to fly south over France before turning South-East over Lake Annecy and, skirting south of the borders of neutral Switzerland, making their run-in to the target. The aircraft reached their turning-point just after midnight, but some time after the main stream had passed southwards, a single aircraft was heard circling in the rainy darkness over the Swiss town of Sion. Its engines were misfiring badly, and it appeared to be attempting to gain height. The aircraft was 467's 'T-Tommy' piloted by 23-year-old Flying Officer Graham Mitchell RAAF. He and his crew were on only their sixth operation together, and in dire trouble. Unable to maintain height, they jettisoned their 4,000 lb 'cookie' and some incendiaries in one last effort to reduce weight. Shortly afterwards PO-T passed low over the hamlet of Thyon, some 6,900 feet above sea level. As it did so it struck high tension wires and smashed into the ground, bursting into flames. The force of the impact scattered wreckage over hundreds of yards, killing all on board. They were buried together two days later at Vevy on Lake Geneva along with a 207 Squadron crew from Langar lost in similar circumstances. The service was swamped by local people wanting to pay their respects. Also attending were the British Air Attaché in Berne, Air Commodore Freddie West VC and the Aga Khan, holidaying nearby.

For those reaching Turin, opposition was negligible. At briefing they had been warned that the weather front forming over France on their outward journey would be sufficiently developed on their return to make a detour out over the Bay of Biscay advisable. It would be dawn by this time, so they were told to keep at nought feet and to formate with other Lancasters if possible to increase fire power in the event of attack by the frequent Ju88 patrols in the area. Flight Lieutenant Bob Gibbs, deputy 'C' Flight commander, and his crew, dodging between the rain squalls, were never seen again. Over England it was a bright summer's morning as the weary survivors made their way back. It was just before 9 o'clock, and Ernie Dring, son of the landlord of Long Bennington's The Wheatsheaf was standing on a hay rick on the edge of the village, already working on the day's harvesting. As the Lancasters circled overhead waiting their turn to land, he was looking up, shielding his eyes against the sun to catch a glimpse of the letter 'W' which would tell him that Pilot Officer John Good had returned. The Aussie and his crew were frequent visitors to his father's pub, and after closing would often accompany the barmaid back to her cottage on Back Lane where they

The crew of 'L–Liz'beth', Bottesford, Spring 1943. Standing, left to right: Sgt W.S. Buchanan, Sgt C.A. Chapman, Sgt J. Greenwood, Sgt W. Bruce, Sgt N.C. Smith. Front: Sgt P. Donlevy, Sgt A.E. Michaels. (C. Allen)

sat talking until the small hours. Ernie would sometimes tag along, but as he now looked upwards, something unusual caught his eye. One of the returning Lancasters had a hole in its fuselage so big that daylight shone through.

In Flying Control the tension was almost tangible. Most of the other aircraft had landed but still nothing had been heard of Mitchell, Gibbs, Good, or Flight Sergeant Chapman. Twenty-year-old 'Sid' Chapman from Melbourne was engaged to a WAAF MT driver on the station named Elizabeth, and constantly flouted the radio procedure by using the callsign 'L-Lizbeth' instead of the usual 'L-London' on his Lancaster, LM311 PO-L. Elizabeth now stood in the corner of the watch office waiting to collect the returning crews and deliver them to debriefing, but as the minutes ticked by, all present were only too aware of her thoughts. Then Chapman's voice came over the R/T. He explained that a flak hit over the target had severed his elevator cables and that he had very little fuel left. Could he attempt a landing using just the trimmer? A hurried discussion made it clear that given the fuel situation there was little alternative but to come in now, and permission was granted. All eyes were on 'Lizbeth' as she joined the circuit and made a steady, shallow approach from the direction of Bennington. Chapman was conscious of the fact that any further stress on the airframe must be avoided, so he waited until the last possible moment to put down the undercarriage. But it was too much. As the locks engaged the tail section separated and fluttered away. In slow motion 'L' reared upwards and stalled, striking the ground nose first a few seconds later. There was a flash, followed a few seconds later by a low rumble and a dirty black pall of smoke, dust and debris. The station fire engine raced out onto the main road but could do nothing. Thirty tons of Lancaster had smeared itself across the field, cutting a swathe in the long grass. There were no survivors, and two days later Arthur Cackett was one of those detailed to escort five flag-draped coffins to Bottesford station where they were loaded on goods waggons, bound for their families in Scotland.

In 1991 a walk across the field in which LM311 crashed revealed an instrument face from the flight engineer's panel, an access panel bearing traces of black paint, and exploded .303 ammunition. A more detailed examination the following year by the Yorkshire Air Museum recovered large quantities of molten aluminium, oil-covered engine components and the pitot tube. On contacting Margaret Butterworth, widow of flight engineer Jack Greenwood, it was revealed that she still had her husband's pocket watch (right). Battered and burnt, it stopped at 8.40 that day in 1943 and has never worked since.

The attack on Turin which had claimed Mitchell, Gibbs and Chapman was the last 'op' of his tour for Johnny Good, and he finished in style. He had lost an engine on the way out, but he and his crew did not want to abort and so jettisoned everything possible to gain enough height to cross the Alps. They went on to bomb the target with such accuracy that they were awarded one of the coveted 'aiming points'. Whilst crossing the Bay of Biscay on the return journey they formated with another Lancaster, obviously in trouble. Good contacted the pilot over the R/T and asked what the problem was. They were a new crew, slightly panicky and low on fuel, so he instructed them to feather an engine and stayed close to give encouragement and advice. As they neared the coast his wireless operator contacted Tangmere and asked permission for their protégé to land. Good declined the invitation to 'pancake' himself, wanting instead to press on for Bottesford and the planned end of tour party. He landed some considerable time after the other crews, and was rewarded with an immediate DFC.

This raid had been extremely traumatic for the Squadron in terms of losses, but they were on the order of battle again on 16th July when five 467 crews joined thirteen others from 5 Group attacking transformer stations in Northern Italy. 467's target was Cislago in the foothills of the Alps. Only the night before, 617 Squadron had failed in its attempt to knock out two similar targets due to thick ground mist in the Alpine valleys. For this second attempt the crews were told not to attack until a 'master of ceremonies' arrived to guide their bombing. Unfortunately he was delayed, which left them orbiting the target for over an hour, giving nightfighters ample opportunity to attack. Pilot Officer Carmichael's aircraft was intercepted by a Ju88, killing his navigator, although they shook off their attacker. Flight Lieutenant Harry Locke in 'O-Orange' decided enough was enough and set course for Spezia docks, the secondary target, and after bombing headed for Blida in North Africa as ordered. Before long dawn had broken, and the African coast was looming ahead, but they were unsure of their precise position, unable to raise Blidaover the radio and very low on fuel. Soon after crossing the coast an aerodrome came into sight, so Locke took what was by now the only option and came in for a landing. His bomb aimer, Frank Townsend wrote:

Unfortunately it was a fighter aerodrome with a 400 yards long runway, so we went through a vineyard, over a deep railway cutting (off with the undercart) and made a perfect pancake. There were no injuries and we were entertained by the French CO. After six days in North Africa we were brought home via Gibraltar, although Tommy Munro (rear gunner) was left behind for a few more days with dysentery. The rest of us came back with Wing Commander Burnett and stayed in Gib overnight where the Wingco filled the Lanc with wine and crates of bananas. He said 'Pray!' as we started to take off. We had 22 bods on board by now, so you can imagine our feelings, as only a few weeks before General Sikorski had gone straight into the drink from the end of the same runway. We flew up the Bay of Biscay in daylight, and for a while the Wingco put the auto-pilot on and came back to play cards! We arrived at Bardney late at night where a 3 ton lorry waited to cart off the Wingco's spoils.

P/O Johnny Good DFC RAAF. Good friends of the landlord of The Wheatsheaf in Long Bennington, Johnny and his crew finished their tour in July 1943 with a trip to Turin, during which they formated with another Lancaster, obviously in difficulties, and shepherded it and its crew to Tangmere and safety. (M. Claridge)

The end of July and the beginning of August saw four raids in quick succession on Hamburg, the largest port in Europe and Germany's second largest city. Although the city had been attacked before on no less than 98 occasions, Sir Arthur Harris considered it was time for it to suffer the full weight of a Bomber Command 'maximum effort'. As a new departure he was allowing his crews to use 'Window' for the first time. This was the codename for the thin strips of tin foil which, when dropped in bundles, would confuse the German radar with spurious signals. With losses running so high it was just the sort of advantage the crews could appreciate, so spirits were high on the night of the first raid, 25/26th July. Sure enough, all of the 467 crews returned safely. On the following night there was a brief return to Essen, the raid inflicting the greatest damage on the Krupps works to date. Although, thanks to 'Window', the German fighters were still reeling and losses on this target were lower than usual, Sergeant Colin Harrison and crew in ED803 PO-Ā suffered a direct hit from flak which knocked out both starboard engines. With no hydraulics the flaps, bomb doors and undercarriage hung useless. Everything removable was thrown out to maintain height, and Jock Robertson, the flight engineer set the engines to a dangerously high 2850 revs, +9 boost. Harrison crash landed at Coltishall where Sergeant Fred Parry, the bomb aimer, recalls that the fighter pilots, having counted 163 holes in the airframe, told him and the rest of the crew that they should be awarded 'Gongs as big as frying pans' for getting her back. As it was, Harrison received an immediate DFM.

The second raid on Hamburg on the night of 27/28th July did not go so well for 467. Flight Sergeant Buchanan and crew, on their first operation, were shot down into the sea with no survivors. Pilot Officer Jim Carrington's crew were on their twelfth operation: two managed to bale out. This was the night of Hamburg's infamous 'Firestorm', brought about by unusually low humidity, high temperatures and an error in Pathfinder marking which moved the aiming point two miles east of the intended target. As it was, bombing around the markers was particularly concentrated, with an estimated 550-600 bomb loads falling in an area of two square miles over a densely packed working class district of the city. By far the most chilling statistic was the 40,000 estimated to have died in the inferno. A further 1.2 million fled the city in the days following this particular raid, a stark testimony to the awesome destructiveness of the bomber.

For the fourth and final attack on 2/3rd August the weather conditions were far from ideal. A thunderstorm meant that the pathfinders were unable to mark, so crews either jettisoned their loads and aborted, or bombed as best they could. Pilot Officer Dave Symonds took his Lancaster down to 6,000 feet over the city, to see through the dense pall of soot and smoke and make an accurate bombing run. They were attacked by a fighter, but managed to evade it without damage, or so they thought. However, there was no answer from the rear gunner, Sergeant B.N. Pratt, and a check revealed that he had been killed by a single bullet to the head. 'Mike' Pratt was buried at St. Swithun's in Long Bennington. David Symonds wrote:

The funeral of Sgt B.N. Pratt at St. Swithun's, Long Bennington. 'Mike' Pratt was killed by a single bullet which entered his turret through the clear vision panel and struck him in the head. (H. Twitchett)

Mike was a cocksparrow of a cockney. When we went for a drink in a crowded bar and I was jostled, Mike would take on the offender with all of his 5'4', and I would have to rescue him from disaster. More importantly, we, the crew had to bury Mike in that grave. Full military honours, rifle shots, the lot. But when we arrived back at Bottesford the hard part started. As we disembarked from our truck the senior WAAF officer called out to me. There was Mike's mother. A tiny figure in black, she walked towards me as I stood rigidly to attention. She took both my hands, and I waited for what? Curses? Instead, and I'll always remember this, she said, 'Mike said, "Don't worry Mum, Skip will always bring me home". Thank you for bringing him home to England'. She released my hands and walked back to the WAAF officers. That Hamburg trip was rough for all my crew, but for me, that little lady from the East End was the hardest.

CHAPTER THIRTEEN

'He will be missed and greatly mourned'

Following the end of the Hamburg raids August 1943 saw a very mixed bag of targets: Cologne, Genoa, Mannheim, Nuremburg and Milan. On a follow-up raid to Milan on the night of 14/15th, Flying Officer Marshall's crew, on only their second 'op', got into difficulties. Problems began when a run-up of the engines a few minutes before take-off revealed a glycol leak. With little time to lose they switched to the spare aircraft, 'Q-Queenie', a battered and uninspiring veteran of many operations. Airborne some minutes behind the rest of the squadron, they were late for the rendezvous off Brighton. Then the flight engineer reported that the temperature on the starboard outer was rising alarmingly. Nevertheless, it was agreed to continue. They avoided two fighter attacks over France by dodging into cloud, but were now lagging further behind. By the time they reached Milan the main force had long gone, and although fires could be seen below there were neither searchlights nor flak. However, no sooner had they begun their bombing run when the gunners called out 'Fighter closing in and firing! Corkscrew starboard — Go!'. Marshall stood the Lancaster on its wingtip, at the same time pushing the nose down sharply. He repeated the manoeuvre until they were at low altitude, and although there was now no sign of the fighter, a second failing engine testified to accuracy of its burst. With only two engines there was now little chance of re-crossing the Alps, besides a fuel tank had been punctured. The only remaining option was to attempt to reach one of the aerodromes in North Africa used in the recent shuttle raid. To add to their problems the navigator had no suitable maps. The wireless operator, 'Ginger' Hallam, remembered:

There followed a period of calm after which I was asked for details of wireless stations in North Africa. After about an hour I commenced wireless transmission with no immediate reply. However, after about two hours of this a station answered HFY, from which I got a QDM — 'course to steer'. The station could have been anywhere south along this course. I remember Bill saying, 'Where is this station, Ginger?', to which I replied, 'I haven't got a clue!'. Bill grumbled 'We could be flying to bloody Fremantle!'. To cut a long story short, the aerodrome was No. 72 Staging Post at Biskra on the edge of the Sahara. There were no night flying facilities there but by plain language communication we arranged for buckets of sand soaked in petrol to be lit on one side of the runway to give us a guide. We landed safely, and when we got out, were of course dressed in blue battledress. Suntanned figures stood around in the half-light wearing khaki drill shorts and we were pounded with questions. 'Where are you from, mate?'. 'Bottesford', 'Where's Bottesford?', 'Near Grantham?'. 'Grantham? Bloody hell! They're from Blighty!'. The story about the fortuitous radio contact was that the operator was a 'ham' at home, and when he couldn't sleep would go up to the radio cabin and search the dial. He came from New Mills in Derbyshire, and we became good friends. It was very fortunate for us!

Biskra was little more than a dirt strip with a handful of tents, so 'Queenie' could not be repaired there. After four weeks of unbearable heat and 'hard tack' biscuits, Marshall and his crew joined a convoy heading for Maison Blanche, Algiers. As Arthur Hallam remarked, it was an eye-opener for a Cheshire lad who had never been further than Blackpool before in his life. At Maison Blanche they collected a Lancaster which had been damaged in the shuttle raids, and from there flew to Rabat, Morocco. On the 25th September they took off for England, but during the flight, icing made the Lancaster uncontrollable. It went into spin and lost several thousand feet before Marshall managed to recover. When they eventually returned to Bottesford they had been away for six weeks, and recognised almost none of the faces on the squadron.

It must have been with some apprehension that Wing Commander Gomm learned on 15th August that Milan was to be the target for the third night running. It always paid to keep the element of surprise, but sometimes two, three or even four visits in succession to the same target were unavoidable. By August 1943 Italian resolve to continue the war was crumbling, and cities such as Milan — containing heavy industry and light defences — presented inviting targets. Dusk on the Sunday evening therefore saw ten 467 Squadron crews bound for Italy, led by Gomm. The last hours of the 15th saw the bomber stream heading southwards over France. The post-raid summaries talked of surprisingly accurate flak near the city of Chartres, and witnesses on 467 apparently saw at least two Lancasters receive direct hits and disintegrate. However, evidence suggests that the losses were actually due to fighters. On board Gomm's ED998 PO-Y a sudden, vicious burst of fire ruptured the fuel tanks and enveloped it in flames. Gomm shouted 'We've been hit! Get out!', but as the crew made frantic attempts to clip on parachutes the Lancaster was torn apart by an explosion which scattered debris over two square miles. At Gomm's side throughout the flight, and for 23 operations beforehand, had been the youngest crew member, James Lee, the 20-year-old flight engineer from Hull. After the explosion he remembered nothing until finding himself floating down under his smouldering parachute. He was falling rapidly, and with badly burned hands could do little to control his descent. Severe injury seemed inevitable when he crashed into a hay rick. Injured and suffering from shock, Lee saw no chance of evasion and decided to give himself up. Painfully he dragged himself to a nearby farmhouse, but the occupants were too afraid of German reprisals to allow him in. This was repeated again before he was eventually taken in by the Paragot family in the town of Chaisnes. At Lee's request they called the local doctor to tend his wounds, knowing that he would inform the Germans. Sure enough Lee spent two weeks in hospital before being transferred to Stalag IVB in Germany. In 1957 he returned to the field where he had landed, at the request of the Paragots who presented him with his parachute and goggles which they had kept. Back in 1943 it had been two months before Lee's mother knew that he was still alive, and her immediate reaction had been to ask for news of the rest of the crew. The squadron adjutant wrote:

Dear Mrs Lee

In reply to your letter I am deeply grieved to have to tell you that the remainder of the crew, without exception, were killed. Your son was the sole survivor.

Wing Commander Gomm was the pilot and captain of the aircraft, as well as the commander of the squadron, and was a pilot and officer of the very highest type. His loss is indeed a heavy one, for we can ill afford to lose men of his ability and charm, and he will be missed and greatly mourned by all those who knew him.

Cosme Gomm and the remaining five members of the crew were buried at St. Désir near Lisieux. In June the citation for Gomm's DSO had ended, '...through his magnificent efforts (he) has built up a Lancaster squadron which is probably second to none'. In support of this the August edition of *5 GroupNews* noted that over the past month 467 had flown the most operational hours within the Group (1178), dropped the greatest tonnage of bombs (710), had the greatest average of serviceable aircraft (21.9) and had produced the greatest number of target photographs (82 out of 163 attempts).

Whilst 467 was coming to terms with Gomm's loss, the post of squadron commander was temporarily filled by 'A' Flight's Squadron Leader A.S. Raphael. The diminutive Londoner was immediately thrown in at the deep end. For weeks now 5 Group's squadrons had been practising 'indirect bombing' techniques at Wainfleet range, carrying out runs at fixed speeds and heights from identifiable landmarks, and dropping bombs on the stopwatch rather than using a bomb sight. Crews guessed that an attack on a precision target was in the offing. Pilot Officer Bill Close, navigator on Flying Officer 'Fish' Whiting's crew wrote:

On the afternoon of 17th August the whole squadron was briefed for a night attack on a place we had never heard of before — Peenemunde — described by the intelligence officer as German Radio Direction Finding Station. We were surprised at this as we knew that all available aircraft of Bomber Command were going to be operating either on this target or on a few others (to create a diversion in the hopes of concealing our main target). The importance of the raid became obvious when the Group Commander himself (Air Vice Marshal Cochrane) paid a lightning visit to the briefing room to give us a pep talk. The main theme of this was that Peenemunde had to be destroyed that night, otherwise we should have to go out nightly until the job was completed. This news did not cheer us at all. Visions of the pitcher and well came before us.

Marie Cooper recalled:

I had a premonition that Raphael would not return as he emerged from the briefing with his usual calm gone, muttering, 'Too many fighters on that route!'. When the rest came out they all looked a bit ruffled and one chap said 'He got more than a bit worked up about the fighters,' and then, shaking his head in an aside 'almost hysterical he was!'.

Raphael's fears were to prove more than justified. The bombers were being sent out despite the fact that it was a moon period, and whilst the moonlight would increase their chances of bombing accurately, it would also make them vulnerable to fighter attack. Peenemunde was being used for the production and testing of V-2 rockets, seen as a serious threat to the progress of any invasion, which therefore had to be eliminated at all costs. 5 Group's crews were told to bomb on the markers if visibility allowed, or if not, to follow their 'indirect' method. Either way, they were to bomb the target. Bill Close recalls that:

We left base just before nine that evening and flew eastwards. The night was clear and at our flying height of 20,000 feet the sky was alarmingly light. Behind, in front, and on each side we could see other bombers, black outlines against the light grey of the sky. It was really no night for night bombers, who rely so much for safety on the cover of darkness. Running over the western end of the Baltic, our bomb aimer, lying in the nose of the aircraft was able to call out accurate ground positions from the map, so clear was the view below. Our turning point, the little island of Bornholm came into view. By now there was a little cloud with more building up to the south. Probably, after all, we should have to bomb blind. Thirty seconds before our time to bomb, however, there was a break in the clouds and the red target indicators were there amongst much smoke and a few fires. So far we were satisfied and relieved, but we were taking no chances. Immediately after the bombs were released the pilot turned sharply to starboard on a north-westerly course and issued a reminder to the gunners to keep their eyes skinned for enemy fighters. Our own return flight was uneventful, but we had the unpleasant sight of seeing many of our bombers being attacked by fighters. Dawn was breaking as we landed after a flight totalling seven hours. All the post-raid reports confirmed the success of the attack, and the heavy price we had to pay for that success.

For 467 the price was indeed heavy, amounting to a fifth of those despatched. A small force of Mosquitoes had been sent to Berlin in order to draw German fighters away, and whilst this initially worked, by the time the third and last wave of attackers arrived, comprised of 5 and 6 Group crews, the defences had recovered and the fighters were waiting for them. Amongst those killed was 'Ray' Raphael. His Lancaster crashed into a lake next to the Peenemunde research station. Of those on board, the rear gunner fell clear and was washed ashore in Poland, and four others including Raphael and Martyn Parry, squadron bombing leader, were recovered from the wreck

F/Sgt Des Sullivan RAAF and members of his air and ground crew sit on a bomb trolley in front of 'their' ED764 'N–Nancy' — or 'Nuts to the Nazis' as the Olive Oyl nose art proclaims. 'Nancy' was shot down over Peenemunde whilst being 'borrowed' by Frank Dixon and crew. (J. Coyne)

and buried locally. After the war they were almost certainly reinterred in the Berlin War Cemetery as 'Unknown Airmen of the 1939–45 War'.

The other loss over Peenemunde was that of Flight Sergeant Frank Dixon RAAF and crew in Lancaster ED764 'N-Nancy'. Soon after completing their bombing run a burst of cannon shells killed the wireless operator and set fire to the port wing. The Germans had recently equipped some of their Messerschmitt 110 nightfighters with upward firing twin cannons so that the fighter could carry out its interception from below, undetected and making full use of the Lancaster's blind spot. This devastating method of attack (called 'Schrage-Musik' - 'Jazz Music') was used for the first time at Peenemunde when six aircraft were accounted for. Bottesford's ED764 therefore has the distinction of being one of the first, if not ***the*** first bomber brought down in this way, but there would be many hundreds more. After the initial attack the surviving crewmembers took to their parachutes, all to became prisoners of war. But this was not quite the end. 'Nancy' was usually flown by Flight Sergeant Des Sullivan RAAF, who takes up the story:

Our crew did three raids to Hamburg in July/August, with an Essen raid in the middle (in my opinion Essen was the toughest target in Germany), but for Peenemunde they gave us the night off. A close friend, Fred Dixon (an Australian) asked if he could borrow our 'N for Nancy' as his own 'plane was playing up. I don't lend golf clubs, tennis racquets or girlfriends, but I reluctantly said 'Yes'. He didn't come back, and I thought he must have got the chop, but 37 years later he called on me when I was administrator of Rottnest Island (off the coast of Australia). As he came down the passage of my residence I recognised him. He held out his hand and said, 'Hello' etc., but I just said, 'Where's my bloody aeroplane?'. I hadn't heard of him since he took off for Peenemunde. I was given a new Lanc, but it wasn't the same as our 'N for Nancy'.

As if this were not enough drama for one night, Warrant Officer 'Pluto' Wilson's ED545 was also attacked soon after leaving the target. The first burst hit the rear turret, knocking it out and putting a round through Sergeant Pat Barry's heel. A fire broke out in the fuselage and the Lancaster went into a steep dive. In the mid-upper turret Sergeant George Oliver from Gedling, Nottinghamshire, continued to fire until the fighter was seen to go down in flames. By now the heat was intense, and ammunition exploding beneath his feet, so Oliver grabbed his parachute and made his way up front with the intention of baling out, collecting the navigator and wireless operator on the way. By now, however, Wilson had managed to control the aircraft, and when told the fuselage was on fire replied, 'Well put the bloody thing out then!' (or words to that effect!). Oliver and the others returned aft and, braving heat and smoke, managed to put out the flames. They then used the fire axe to free Pat Barry from the wrecked turret. Pat Barry said:

As regards the raid, I spent all of the return journey on the rest bed, and I remember five or six of my colleagues coming in at intervals to talk to me, and each said, I think, 'Cheer up, we're just crossing the coast'. Well, we had to cross three coasts, two of Denmark's and the U.K.'s one — but six? That was too much! After returning to base I went first to the sick bay and was then transferred to Rauceby. After about a month I went to East Grinstead for plastic surgery, and of course to become a 'Guinea Pig', but I never flew operationally again. We always considered Pluto flew like an angel after a pint or two. When we were dressed for battle he called me 'Mister Five by Five', '...he's five feet tall and five feet wide!'. I always carried a personal bomb load, maybe a half brick or some such thing to throw through the clear vision panel as a parting gift when leaving the target.'

As the only married man on the crew George Oliver had more to lose than most, but as their Lancaster fell out of the sky his only thought had been to shoot down their attacker. For this act of determination he was awarded the Conspicuous Gallantry Medal, second only to the Victoria Cross in order of precedence. In addition Pluto Wilson received an immediate DFC, and when the crew finished their tour three weeks later the other five members each received a DFM. This made them the most decorated first-tour crew on 467, a record still standing when the Squadron was disbanded in 1945.

Sgt Pat Barry, rear gunner on the crew of 'Pluto' Wilson outside Buckingham Palace following the investiture for his DFM. A volunteer from neutral Eire, he was so badly wounded over Peenemunde, he never flew operationally again. (P. Barry)

CHAPTER FOURTEEN

On a Wing and a Prayer

After the Squadron's mauling over Peenemunde, August 1943 had yet more surprises in store. The first came just two days after the raid when Wing Commander J.R. Balmer RAAF was posted in from nearby Syerston to take over command of the Squadron — a command held by 'Ray' Raphael for just 48 hours. Short and stocky, he was 467's first Australian CO. 'Sam' Balmer had no lack of determination or guts, but as with Gomm this was to prove no insurance and luck was ultimately to elude him. He was killed in action in May 1944 on the last raid of his second tour.

The second surprise of the month was provided by the news that Gracie Fields was to visit the aerodrome. Plays and concerts were always well attended, and because they were thought good for morale, no effort was spared with, for example an ENSA concert party putting on an extra matinée performance of Noel Cowerd's *This Happy Breed* for crews taking part in the attack on Peenemunde. Naturally, artistic temperament sometimes reared its head. When on one occasion the station's unofficial dance band went on strike over pay (or the lack of it), the entertainments officer sent an airman to Nottingham with instructions to buy an amplifier and a stock of 78s with strict tempo dance tunes. The disgruntled prima donnas soon got the message and returned to work! But now that Bottesford had hit the big time in the world of entertainment extra special preparations had to be made. A makeshift stage was hastily erected in one of the hangars and decorated with red, white and blue streamers and flags, and the floors were cleaned with 100 octane fuel (which successfully removed the oil stains but left a distinctly heady aroma). In the meantime the station was scoured for seating and the catering officer began preparing a special buffet in honour of the occasion. Ron Shaw recalled:

My wife, being a Lancashire lass, was most interested when Gracie Fields visited the aerodrome. Gracie came from Rochdale, my wife from Burnley. One of Gracie's songs, quite popular at the time was 'Coming in on a Wing and a Prayer'. My wife came to the 'drome that day, went into my office, and then into the hangar. That night she watched the Squadron taking off for Berlin. We thought ops were off, but they weren't, and she was near enough to the runway to be able to wave to some of the crews. She regards that as one of her lovely memories, and fortunately that night they all came back. Squadron Leader Gibbs said 'You'd better bring your wife more often if it'll bring the aircraft back!'.

'On a wing and a prayer' — Gracie Fields gives a concert in one of Bottesford's hangars, 31st August 1943. Officers sit in chairs, 'erks' hand from the ceiling, and fourteen disgruntled crews are sent to attack Berlin! (W.R. Baguley)

The eight crews rostered were far from happy to be missing the show, and with Berlin as their target, who could blame them? Inside the hangar some of the erks had risked life and limb to obtain a good view by climbing the girders reinforcing the hangar walls. There was a strong contingent from the RASC depot in Bottesford village as well as other aerodromes, and bicycles littered the approach to the hangar into which it was later estimated that over 1500 people had been packed.

Now that the weather was better, the number of outdoor diversions to be enjoyed on a rest period or stand-down had increased dramatically. Those on the station had been given the freedom to roam the grounds of Belvoir Castle, including the use of the reservoir for swimming. Bicycles, as ever, were a much sought-after commodity in allowing one to get 'out and about', but even without bikes, the more resourceful members of the station could always find something to amuse them. Few would disagree that for sheer physical effort the armourers had one of the hardest jobs on the aerodrome, so for them days off were an opportunity to do as little as possible. Aubrey Tongue of 'C' Flight remembered:

There were no ops on this particular day, it was nice and warm, and I was one of the lucky ones to be stood down after dinner. I had about enough cash to buy ten fags and a cuppa, so thought I'd catch up on some reading and writing in the 'afto', then go to the camp cinema after tea — provided I could borrow a 'tanner'! In the billet on 5 Site there were seven or eight of us in the same plight, with the usual small talk, i.e. what we'd do if we came into some money. The hut was thick with smoke, and being armourers there were a few guns knocking around, P14s, 17s, SMLEs, Stens together with a goodly number of rounds (Allsorts-Bassetts!). Boredom soon crept in, various activities were proposed, but alas, no enthusiasm. Then, out of the blue I asked a simple question. Would a 9mm Sten round go through the thickness of the three doors in the billet if fired from one end to the other? I was told to either try it or to wrap up, so I tried it. It went straight through and took out a lump of brickwork! After the usual remarks regarding parentage and lunacy, one or two of the other bods got their guns and went outside, and soon five or six of us were loosing off at an oil drum eighty yards away on the brow of the hill. Quite a lot of ammo was used in the exercise, but the enemy needn't have feared, because the drum was hit only five times or so! After a quarter of an hour the shooting stopped and we went back inside, at which point Alex Alexander, an armourer from next door came in to tell us that a Sergeant and three Corporal S.P.s had arrived on the site. Next Corporal Sond came in to say the S.P.s were investigating reports of shooting on 5 Site! Eventually our hut was visited and we had to produce our guns for one of the Corporals to see whether they had been fired. He duly reported to his Sergeant that NONE of the weapons had been used, and after a few tremulous minutes (it seemed hours), the 'Imperial Guard' upped and went.

Later we were told that the Military Police had been called by a farmer who had reported bullets flying around his farmhouse like hornets. It turned out his farm was on the other side of the hill, behind and below our target! Word had it that the thick S.P. (who had only to sniff the guns to know that they had been fired) was not so thick and had acted in this way to save us going on a 'fizzer'. We also thought the Sergeant turned a blind eye, because nothing more was heard — apart from much muttering in the Armoury!

As well as the first autumn chills, September brought a continuation of attacks on German targets. Whilst the effects of raids could be variable, in one area at least the results were more predictable: casualties. On the 4th, Flight Lieutenant Carmichael, Pilot Officer Turner and their crews fell victim to the 'Big City'. On the 24th Mannheim claimed the crews of Pilot Officers Farmer and Long. All four captains died with their aircraft, in Farmer's case holding the aircraft steady so that five of his crew could take to their parachutes. As an illustration of how difficult it was to get out of a damaged Lancaster at night and in bulky flying gear, of the 29 crewmen on board the four Lancasters, these five were the only survivors.

Towards the end of September 'B' Flight received a replacement aircraft which was to earn itself a special place not only on the Squadron, but in the history of Bomber Command. On arrival at Bottesford Lancaster I R5868 had already completed 68 operations with 83 Squadron as 'Q-Queenie'. Soon re-christened 'S-Sugar', today she is preserved as the centrepiece of the Bomber Command museum, Hendon, having ended the war as the RAF's

Sgts Steve Bethell and Albert Martin pose in front of what is thought to be 'S–Sugar' on her Bottesford dispersal, October 1943. 'Sugar' completed 137 sorties, making her the second highest scorer in the RAF, and can now be seen at the Bomber Command Museum, Hendon. (S. Bethell)

second highest scoring Lancaster with 137 successful sorties to her credit. Back in 1943 'Sugar' was viewed with far less respect. She flew her first operation with the Squadron on the night of 27/28th September piloted by Alan Finch, who complained that he thought her fit only for training. Two nights later it was Neale McClelland's turn. Ken Worden, his mid-upper gunner remembers:

We had not been at Bottesford long when we were allocated a new Lancaster, straight from the manufacturer's. We did one or two trips in it before it was taken from us and given to a Pathfinder squadron. I imagine their need was greater than ours! We were then given another Lancaster from the same squadron which had just returned from a Maintenance Unit after a major overhaul. On our first trip to Bochum, instead of climbing to 20,000 feet to bomb we could only reach 17,000, which didn't please us much. Neale complained about it the next day, but we still had to use it. We did five more trips in it and then went on leave. In the meantime the aircraft was not allowed to stand idle and another crew flew it to Berlin where it was in a collision over the target. They managed to get it home but it was extensively damaged and sent to an M.U. We didn't see it again for another 30 odd years.

The need to make good losses, battle damage and wear and tear led to a constant flow of aircraft. To prevent further strain on already overworked engineering sections, severely damaged Lancasters or those awaiting their 500 hours major inspection were broken down into sections, placed on trailers and driven to specialist civilian repair depots. Here spares were combined with cannibalized sections to produce complete airframes. By the end of the war 3,816 aircraft had been refurbished in this way and in 1943 alone 55% of the Lancasters supplied were 'retreads'. One of four Avro repair depots had been opened at Bottesford's satellite, Langar, in 1942. However, despite the good work done by repair depots, the Ministry of Aircraft Production recognised the advisability of effecting as many repairs on home airfields as possible. With this in mind between 1942 and 1944 all heavy bomber stations were provided with one of the larger B1 type hangars and their own civilian working parties. Bottesford's new B1 was situated next to the firing butts across the Normanton/Bennington road. Rather than close the road completely to traffic, level crossing type gates were installed.

Soon afterwards construction also began on three new T2 hangars on the technical site. Along with 23 other bomber aerodromes, Bottesford had been chosen to house some of the growing number of assault gliders being stockpiled for the invasion of Europe. Being constructed largely of spruce, plywood and canvas the 32 Horsa gliders delivered were deemed unsuitable for outside storage, hence the provision of additional hangar space. However, until the hangars were completed the gliders were staked down across the landing ground. It was one of these that Pilot Officer Roberts almost 'collected' whilst taking off for Munich on October 2nd. Roberts' Lancaster veered off the runway and bounced across the grass at 80 mph. He narrowly missed a Horsa but finally managed to pull up after some frantic snaking, which was no joke with 2,000 gallons of fuel and 12,000 lbs of high explosives and incendiaries on board. After a hurried inspection by flashlight he was allowed to come round again and have another go, fortunately this time without incident. That same night, after an otherwise uneventful trip Pilot Officer K.A. McIver DFC and crew in ED530 O-Orange noticed that the fuel was running very low, and at approximately 0150 hours they ditched 25 miles off Beachy Head. Some time later that morning Flight Sergeant McGrath was picked up drifting in the emergency dinghy, the only survivor.

A few weeks after the arrival of 'S-Sugar' another 'celebrity' had followed her to Bottesford, 24-year-old Squadron Leader Rollo Kingsford-Smith RAAF, posted in to take over command of 'B' Flight from Keith Sinclair who had finished his tour. He was the nephew of pioneering aviator Air Commodore Sir Charles Kingsford-Smith of 'Southern Cross' fame.

As autumn gradually gave way to winter, diversions due to the weather, particularly fog, began to be more commonplace. Seventeen 467 crews returning from Stuttgart on the morning of the 8th received a signal from Group diverting them to Tangmere. However, when later that same morning orders came through from Bomber Command HQ at High Wycombe to provide aircraft for a raid on Hanover that night, 467 found that it could only muster four fresh crews. 207 Squadron at Langar, on the other hand, had more air crews than serviceable aircraft, so S-Sugar was borrowed by their Pilot Officer Barnett for the night. Sergeant Colin Campbell, the mid-upper gunner on fellow Australian Bruce Simpson's crew recalls that particular raid well:

During the run-in Bruce saw something ahead and instinctively pulled back on the stick. We felt a thump, and then an avalanche of air, and looking down over the starboard beam I saw a twin engined aircraft diving steeply away. It seems that a part of that aircraft had struck our bomb aimer's position, taking with it the perspex bubble and the bomb sight. Ken, the bomb aimer, was hurled backwards and showered with perspex. The nav, Roy, had his charts and equipment blown away and his oxygen tube disconnected so that he had to hold it in his mouth to breathe. I looked forward to see a head sticking out of the fuselage. I thought at first that the astrodome had been smashed and that Snowy, the wireless operator, was looking out. But as I watched he climbed further and further out. I called to Roy who shouted to him, but it would have been impossible to hear with the noise of the wind blowing through the hatch. The next moment he came bowling along the top of the fuselage. I ducked as he struck the turret a glancing blow and out of the corner of my eye saw him go over the tail turret. Both myself and Taffy, the rear gunner, saw Snowy's chute going down behind us, and a crew later reported that they had seen a parachute coned by searchlights at about this time and place.

By now we had lost height from 19,500 to 18,000 feet, so Bruce decided to go back through the target area as it was the quickest way home. Roy remembered the course out and we weaved towards the coast. Monica was pipping all the way and I was bursting to relieve myself. Bruce, Roy and Charlie were all frozen, but Ken was better clothed and got up into the front turret, sitting above the hole until we were in the circuit. I tried to relieve myself, but with frozen hands — too late. A miserable time from then on. We couldn't find a place to land. Bruce was about to climb to 5,000 feet and lob us out, but Roy managed to fix our position as just off the Humber and gave a course to fly. Then Ken spotted a lit aerodrome (Grimsby), and we made for it calling 'Darkie'. We received permission to pancake and Taffy and I took up crash positions in case the undercarriage was damaged. We spent the night in hospital and subsequently found that we had brought the 'Cookie' back. The next afternoon Group Captain McKechnie flew over with Lewis's crew to take us back to Bottesford. Roy and Bruce went to Rauceby with frostbite where they spent some weeks as walking wounded, enjoying the hospitality of Bert and his wife at the White Hart in Sleaford. They were subsequently awarded a DFC each.'

Unfortunately, 467's time at Bottesford was to draw to a close with a reminder, if any were needed, that experience was no insurance against misfortune. On the 20th October eight crews took part in a raid on Leipzig, an attack at extreme range not helped by a weather front forming over the target area. Whilst still an hour west of Leipzig, Pilot Officer Ernie Fayle's Lancaster was attacked by two fighters. The rear gunner returned fire and claimed hits, and that was the last of them. However, danger was still close at hand.

In the murk a nervous gunner in another Lancaster mistook them for a fighter and let fly. Fayle's bomb aimer was wounded, an oil pipe was severed, flooding the fuselage, and the instruments rendered useless. At the same time the Lancaster rolled onto its back and fell 3,000 feet before Fayle managed to regain control, going on to bomb the target despite a windscreen covered in ice and a rear gunner unconscious through oxygen starvation. As the raid summary put it, 'Bombs were jettisoned all over Germany. Not at all a successful raid — far from it. Today was a stand-down. It will give the boys a chance to recover after yesterday's hectic do.'

But the recovery period was a short one, for on the 22nd 569 'heavies' attacked Kassel, 15 of them from Bottesford. Despite early problems with marking there was a sufficient concentration of bombs for a fire storm to break out in the city centre, causing extensive damage and thousands of casualties. But the raiders also paid a heavy penalty and were harried to and from the target by nightfighters. Forty-three failed to return, among which were 467's Gerry Godwin and crew, shot down into the sea. They had been on their 27th operation, just three short of finishing. Weather brought about a succession of 'scrubs' over the next few days until November 3rd which saw a return to the Ruhr, this time Dusseldorf. It was another heavy raid, with over five hundred aircraft taking part. Squadron Leader Bill Lewis and his crew had been posted in from 44 Squadron in July so that Lewis could take command of 467's 'C' Flight. At 1700 hours on November 3rd they took off with the rest of the Squadron for Dusseldorf on what was to be their tenth operation since arrival. Two hours later they were crossing Belgium at around 18,000 feet when they received a flak hit in the bomb bay, setting it on fire. Struggling for control, Lewis gave the order to abandon the aircraft. Sergeant Ron Morley, the 22-year-old wireless operator from Leicester, left his position and made for the forward escape hatch. As he passed the pilot, Lewis took a hand off the control column and gave a thumbs-up for encouragement. Thinking all was well, Morley followed the engineer and bomb aimer out through the hatch. Taken in by the Resistance, he was smuggled across Belgium, France and eventually arrived back in England on 29th December to discover that the Squadron had since moved to Waddington, and that Lewis and the two air gunners had died in the burning Lancaster. He recalls that his family really had something to celebrate that New Year. His escape had been miraculous, he and the Navigator, F/Sgt Garvey, being the only airmen out of the hundreds to be shot down flying from Bottesford to successfully evade capture and make it back to Britain. Nevertheless, Morley's escape almost went wrong when, on a crowded railway station in Paris, he accidentally bumped into a German soldier and exclaimed without thinking 'Christ! Sorry mate!'. Fortunately the German was too preoccupied to take much notice.

467 had been warned at the start of November that it would be moved to Waddington once work had been completed on the new runways there. There were no complaints, for as 207 Squadron knew, Waddington was a much cleaner, warmer, more comfortable pre-war station close to the delights of

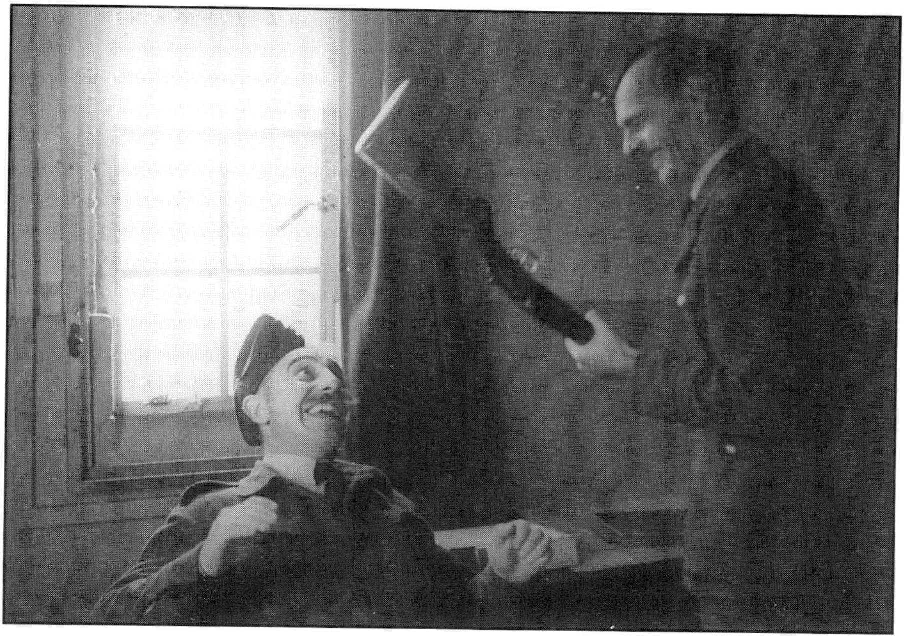

'C' Flight's S/Ldr Bill Lewis finds himself in a spot of bother with Keith Sinclair, his opposite number on 'B' Flight! Lewis and his crew were the last operational losses at Bottesford, failing to return from Dusseldorf in November 1943. (V. Howarth)

Lincoln. Work in moving equipment to the Squadron's new home began on November 10th, not helped by the fact that operations were scheduled for that night. The target, Modane, was a large railway junction on the French side of the Franco/Italian border. Sixteen of the seventeen Bottesford crews available managed to take off, although one returned early due to engine failure. The remainder found the target easily, and with no flak, fighters, or searchlights to distract them they were able to inflict considerable damage, borne out by the fact that all were awarded 'aiming points' after the raid. This was to prove the Squadron's last raid from Bottesford, for on the 12th they began moving to Waddington where they remained until the end of the European war. On the day that the Squadron moved to Waddington their 'C' Flight was detached to form the nucleus of a new sister squadron, 463. Bill Lewis had originally been told that the Squadron would be his, but his loss meant that command went instead to Rollo Kingsford-Smith. Group Captain McKechnie became commanding officer of the newly opened Metheringham, taking with him several members of the Intelligence Section. He was killed in January 1944 flying with a 106 Squadron crew, ignoring, as ever, the order not to fly on operations.

CHAPTER FIFTEEN

A Friendly Invasion

On September 3rd 1943 U.S. Secretary of State Cordell Hull and Britain's Viscount Halifax finally agreed that, in return for the vast amounts of arms and material Britain was receiving in war aid, additional airfields would be made available to the U.S. Army Air Force in the U.K. for its escalating campaign over Europe. As part of this process, in late 1943 ten airfields in the Grantham/Newark area were relinquished to the Troop Carrier Command of the United States Ninth Army Air Force, elements of which had begun arriving in Britain from October onwards in preparation for the coming invasion of Europe. For the allies airborne operations were still in their infancy, and in the coming months the task of the Troop Carrier Command would be to acclimatise themselves to European weather, whilst practising paratroop and supply drops, glider towing, constantly refining their tactics in the light of experience. As the RAF 5 Group bombers moved eastwards into Lincolnshire, the Group's Headquarters in Grantham was taken over by the IXth AAF Command and the area's 'friendly invasion' began in earnest.

Following U.S. custom Bottesford became 'Station 480'. Its first unit was one of the oldest in the Ninth, the 50th Troop Carrier Wing, which had been formed in early 1941. They had transported supplies across America, Alaska and the Caribbean before moving overseas in September 1943. Now a training unit, they arrived at Cottesmore in October, and a month later received orders to move to Bottesford along with the 336th Signal Company. After the relative comfort of Cottesmore's pre-war barracks and mess halls, Bottesford presented an entirely different picture. Nonetheless, the general opinion was that the hutted accommodation compared favourably with that found in the States. However, as winter made its presence felt this view was modified! Within a week of arrival it was Thanksgiving Day, the first in the 'European Theater of Operations' for most of the men, and despite the outward joviality, thoughts of home were inevitably very much to the fore. As they looked around them many of the young Americans must have wondered just what it was there was to be thankful for. A good many of them were farm boys, deliberately chosen by the Air Corps because of their familiarity with big machinery, but although they now found themselves in a rural backwater, there was nothing familiar about the environment, except maybe that it resembled '...something out of a Hollywood murder mystery'. Homesick, young and unsure of themselves, their first brushes with the locals were far from reassuring. Not only were the accents hard to understand, but far from being grateful for 'pulling their chestnuts out of the fire',

Captain Hugh J. Nevins, the 50th Troop Carrier Wing's glider officer, in the cockpit of his personal C–47 'War Weary'. (F. Ehrman)

many English people seemed aloof and resentful of their presence. There were, fortunately, a few exceptions. Bottesford's HF transmitting station on Sewstern Lane remained in RAF hands throughout the time the Americans were there, and its operatives were a part of the small RAF 'care and maintenance' party under the command of Squadron Leader Pearl. AC1 Bob Williamson wrote:

We at the HF transmitting station suddenly began to live in comparative luxury. Our food supply had changed from English stodge to tinned ham, chicken, peanut butter, a great assortment of tinned fruit as well as lots of 'cookies', all in tins weighing about 10 lbs. We had never had it so good. Not long after the arrival of the Americans it was Thanksgiving Day, and all the RAF personnel were invited to their mess hall where we had a fantastic banquet, and after nearly four years of rationing we had nearly forgotten that such a wide variety of food existed! It was just before this that I received a call from the Entertainments Officer, who asked if I could operate movie projectors. This was a real coincidence because I'd befriended the civilian cinema manager who sometimes left me running the show whilst he popped over to the NAAFI to quench his thirst. I was told that he'd run off with the cash from the cinema and a girl from the NAAFI, and did I think I could keep the shows running? I'd receive an ex-gratia payment of £2-10s-0d a week..! It was usual in those days to show a travelogue before the movie, and this particular evening it was about Chicago. At the end of the show there was a knock on the projection box door and I opened it to find an American. He asked if I'd re-run the travelogue as it showed his home and the street where he lived. We waited until everyone had gone and he went back to the auditorium and watched to his heart's content. I often wonder if he made it back.

The 50th TCW only operated a handful of aircraft itself, mostly for training or communications, although by the end of December it had on strength three twin engined C-53D Curtiss Commando transports, a small twin-engined Cessna UC78 'Bobcat' communications aircraft, two former RAF Percival Proctors and an Airspeed Oxford II. Also present was a single Waco CG4A assault glider. Nevertheless, the Bottesford circuit was always busy with Douglas C-47 'Skytrain' transports belonging to the 434th and 435th Troop Carrier Groups based at Fulbeck and Langar, and the 315th TCG from Welford Park in Berkshire. All three came under the command of the 50th TCW. Following a practice drop of the 101st Airborne Division in December, the three units spent most of their time ferrying hospitalized U.S. troops from Northern Ireland to the mainland. Three days before Christmas the 810th Medical Air Evacuation Squadron (Transport) arrived at Bottesford with its own C-47s to continue the work. These flights took place on an increasing scale, and their importance was acknowledged in February when a team of forty newsmen arrived to take part in a medical evacuation flight between Maghaberry in Northern Ireland and Pershore in Worcestershire. The subsequent article in the U.S. forces newspaper *Stars and Stripes* read:

Ready to Carry Invasion Wounded

With the disclosure yesterday of details of the flying hospital wards which will evacuate wounded from second front battle areas, it was revealed that the Ninth Air Force has a separate Troop Carrier Command operating in the British Isles. The first complete air evacuation group ever organized for the sole purpose of carrying wounded men is ready and waiting in England to transport thousands of Allied casualties a day from the invasion battlefields of the continent to secure hospitals in the British Isles.

On the day of the invasion there will be a large number of evacuation squadrons with the Ninth Air Force Troop Carrier Command, USSTAF officials revealed yesterday. Each squadron is comprised of 13 transport planes, each capable of carrying 18 litter patients. There is one surgeon to a flight of six planes and a nurse and enlisted surgical technician aboard every plane.

At present 200-300 sick soldiers are being taken every week from hospitals in Ireland to hospitals in England which have been set up to handle invasion casualties and are at present almost empty. For the air evacuation group the three planes they send to Ireland every day is routine training for the job ahead.

The nurses and enlisted technicians work as a team in one of the Army's unique enlisted/commissioned relationships. A typical team is the Jones/Marshall combina-

Lieutenant Joshua D. Logan of the 50th Troop Carrier Wing's A–2 Section (Intelligence), painting a room at Wing Headquarters. After the war Logan found fame as director of the film *South Pacific* and co-writer of the musical *Paint Your Wagon*. (F. Ehrman)

tion. The nurse is 2/Lt. Naomi N. Jones of Hamilton, Texas, and the surgical technician is S/Sgt George Marshall of Pittsburgh. Lt. Jones is a very pretty little girl with a cute, turned up nose, all of which belies her six years' nursing experience. For a year after she completed her three year course she practised nursing in Texas and then, two years ago, joined the Army Nurse Corps. She is neither married nor engaged.

Marshall is a big, rough looking boy who looks as if he might have been on the Pittsburgh police force. He was. Before he joined the Army he spent eight years as a Pittsburgh cop and later, a detective. He has been married for seven years. 'Jonesy is the best there is,' says Marshall of his diminutive working companion. 'Jonesy' on the other hand, claims that 'my sergeant' is the finest surgical technician in the group.

Military planners estimated that the invasion of Europe was going to be extremely costly in casualties. Medical care in the field was always rough and ready, so if casualties could be evacuated to hospitals in Britain, not only would their chances of survival be increased, but it would prevent the invasion bridgehead becoming clogged with wounded who might slow replacement men and equipment. This was vital if the pressure was to be maintained. With such a burden of responsibility Christmas offered few opportunities for rest or relaxation. The Wing records remarked:

Christmas Eve was but another day of duty at Wing and Maneuver Headquarters, and except for a special Christmas eve candle light communion service conducted by Major Floyd S. Smith, Wing chaplain, at 2200 hours in the base chapel, the Fiftieth marked its first Yuletide season overseas at work. Chaplain Smith arranged for Christmas Day liberty runs to Newark cathedral, allowing personnel to attend a special Christmas Day worship service, and conducted services in the station chapel for officers and men unable to make the trip. All sections functioned as on any other day.'

The reason for the heightened activity over Christmas was explained on January 7th when C-47s of the 81st Troop Carrier Squadron, 436th Troop Carrier Group began to arrive at Bottesford direct from the U.S.A. On January 1st the 436th's ground echelon had been at Camp Shanks, New York. On the 21st they embarked on the Queen Mary and arrived at Gourock in Scotland a week later. The following day a troop train took them via Glasgow, Edinburgh, Newcastle and pulled in at Bottesford station in the early hours of the 30th where a convoy of trucks was waiting to ferry them to the airfield and a waiting meal. In comparison the air echelons had been widely spread, with — for example — the 436th's commanding officer Lieutenant Colonel Adriel N. Williams commanding a flight at Borinquen Field, Puerto Rico. Williams' flight's journey to Britain involved stop-offs at Waller Field (Trinidad), Belem and Natal in Brazil, and on the night of January 6th a 1448 mile 'hop' across the Atlantic to Ascension Island. On the following day the flight flew 1370 miles further east to Roberts Field, Liberia. From here the next destinations were Rufisque, French West Africa and Marrakech, French West Morocco. Finally on the 18th January they set out for Prestwick in Scotland, making a wide detour out over the Atlantic to avoid German air activity. They reached Bottesford on the 21st. According to records several crews had eventful journeys:

Lieutenant Richard J. Wilson perhaps had more difficulty than any other pilot, as the trim of his ship was at all times unstable, either nose heavy or tail heavy, due to Major Herman (no middle initial) Finklestein's rushing about in taking pictures, or his looking for his hat, his jacket, his K-rations, his face powder or his tooth brush.'

Another pilot to suffer during the flight from Marrakech to St. Mawgan was Captain John F. Wallen Junior of the 81st TCS. Way out over the Atlantic he sighted a German Junkers 88 on patrol. Since the C-47s carried no armament with which to defend themselves, he ducked into the nearest available cloud. After a suitable time he emerged to find himself caught in a frantic engagement between an RAF Coastal Command Liberator and a U-Boat. The subsequent manoeuvre which, according to records he executed 'with great efficiency' was described as 'Getting the Hell away!'.

Throughout February the weather was poor. Although six British Horsa gliders were issued to the 436th for evaluation only 64.55 hours were flown throughout the month, meaning that glider pilots were forced to fly as co-pilots on the C-47s in order to keep their hands in. This was the first time that many of the Americans had encountered the Horsa. It was a large aircraft, could carry a maximum of twenty eight troops and two pilots, and had a maximum all-up weight of 15,250 lbs. Its huge flaps allowed it to make an extremely steep descent, something remarked upon by the pilots of the 81st TCS who found this hard to get used to. As time went by, increasing numbers of civilian carpenters were employed in modifying the Horsas to American specifications, and in assembling the CG4A Wacos which were being shipped from the States in huge wooden packing crates. Corporal Ron Shaw, now on the RAF care and maintenance party, remembered that the Americans were generous enough to donate one of the Waco packing crates to the station's RAF cricket team. It was transported to the green at nearby Staunton Harold, used by the team to play fixtures against other RAF stations. The case was converted into a pavilion and changing room as a token of appreciation to the village for use of the pitch, and so that it could be used by local men when they returned from the war.

Because there were now four squadrons in residence in addition to the almost constant flow of aircraft from the other units, ten new 'loop' type hardstandings were added to the original forty 'frying pans' already available. The new dispersals were of a design employed by the USAAF on their heavy bomber bases and considered superior to their RAF counterparts in that aircraft could manoeuvre more easily on them. Waterlogging and low temperatures delayed construction so the problem of congestion was temporarily solved by laying sections of Pierced Steel Planking, a prefabricated

Formation of C-47 transports of the 81st Troop Carrier Squadron, 436th Troop Carrier Group, 1944. (M. Wolfe)

track of interlocking pressed steel panels developed for use on temporary airstrips. So durable was PSP that sections can still be seen around the airfield today.

Throughout the winter, the small RAF care and maintenance party relieved the boredom by throwing itself with gusto into 5 Group sporting activities, a task in which it was fully supported by the Americans who provided transport. They were more relaxed than the RAF in this respect, and it was always possible to hitch a ride on the courier planes which left Bottesford twice daily for the south coast. The Americans seemed more informal in other ways too. A good example was the flying control officer who insisted on being called 'Al', after the character he had played in a film with ice skating star Sonje Henje before the war. Ron Shaw saw a G.I., cigar in mouth, stop his sweeping one morning to shout across to the American Colonel coming out of headquarters, 'Mornin' Colonel!'. Rather than rebuke him, the Colonel merely paused long enough to remove his own cigar, growled 'Mornin' Son!', put the cigar back in, and strode away; it could never have happened in the RAF!

CHAPTER SIXTEEN

'Git thar fustest with the mostest'

Throughout the first half of 1944 American records show that the 50th TCW's medical section maintained a 'very popular' prophylactic station in Nottingham's Red Cross building in an effort to keep men free from venereal disease. For those ignorant of the warnings an early treatment room was set up in the SSQ, wherein the most popular reading matter was a special notebook containing the names and addresses of the ladies deemed responsible for spreading the infection! At one point in 1944 the problem became so alarming that both Nottingham and Grantham were placed out of bounds to U.S. servicemen. Throughout the war troops of all nationalities flooded into Nottingham, drawn by its pubs and its reputation as 'the city of pretty women', but where there were servicemen there were inevitably also rich pickings for prostitutes. However, most females encountered in the pubs and dance halls simply wanted to forget their drab wartime existence for a while. Amongst the Troop Carrier Groups, it was common knowledge that they were expendable and expected to take upwards of fifty percent casualties in the coming invasion; so many young men, although usually shy and retiring were tempted to live life to the full in their rare moments off — before it was too late. The following extract from the 81st Troop Carrier Squadron monthly history is worth quoting in its entirety:

February was a dull and depressing month for the entire squadron. At first sight, the men liked England in general and the camp in particular. The barracks were better than many of the men had occupied in the States; the food was superior to any that could be found in the surrounding towns. Within a few days, however, the barracks proved, also, to be colder and damper than those in the States, and the food took an undesired drop in quality. Another shock came when an order was issued for the men to turn in their arms. All of the build up to war that had taken place during the squadron's training period suddenly crashed to the ground in ruins. When the men had to relinquish their guns, they felt that once more they were being treated like rookies instead of soldiers. Other 'beefs' the men had were the slowness of mail delivery, the bad weather, with rain and mud most of the time, extra KP and guard duties, English beer and the lack of Whiskey, and a hundred more minor items. Possibly beneath it all were two basic reasons: homesickness and a lack of activity, but even though these might be considered, morale continued to drop.'

As usual, the inactivity was caused by the low cloud, rain and snow which covered Britain throughout January and February 1944. In consequence the 81st Troop Carrier Squadron only managed 425 hours flying in February as opposed to 1,240 back in October. The time was spent instead learning RAF and USAAF air traffic control and radio procedures, and in carrying out aerodrome defence exercises with the Home Guard. However, the 81st TCS's history records that the most difficult task was:

...convincing the vehicle drivers that the British really did drive on the left hand side of the road. On the social side well developed European Theater of War coughs didn't prevent most of the personnel from enjoying 48 hour passes in London, Glasgow or Edinburgh. Frequent visits to Nottingham enabled even the more sedate members of the squadron to enjoy the mundane pleasures of the Palais de Danse. Some very pleasant contacts were made. The knack of drinking warm and well-watered beer was easily acquired, although Scotch at £3-10s (a bottle) went down a little slower. Outside of the weather, life in the E.T.O. has not been too rough, although the British are endangering international relations with their medieval plumbing systems, or lack of same. The squadron theme song is now 'Honeybucket Rose'.

Martin Wolfe, a radio operator in the 81st TCS, wrote in his excellent book, *Green Light: Men of the 81st Troop Carrier Squadron Tell their Story*:

Before many days at Bottesford, our sour mood began to colour our assessment of the British people. Even before we had a chance to meet and talk with them, prejudices and clichés about life in Britain began to jell. For example: there were the British workers on the base whose duty it was to maintain the taxiing strips and runways. One of them handled an ancient steamroller which became a kind of symbol of 'Limey' ineptitude and addiction to moss-covered customs. Most of the time that steamroller would just sit there in the rain. Once in a while, when the weather cleared, you could see the worker who handled it up on the steamroller's seat, emptying another mug of tea from his thermos. Then, whether he had actually driven it or not, he would carefully shine up the large manufacturer's plate on the boiler stack. This steamroller had a sort of Toonerville Trolley device for a pressure governor: two brass balls revolving in a stand near the gauge. When the British worker finished polishing his brass plate, darned if he didn't begin polishing those brass balls. He and his shiny brass balls became the object of some pretty sarcastic comments.'

Private First Class Frank Ehrman, a clerk in the headquarters of the 50th TCW had arrived in October 1943. He recalled:

We stayed at this 'mud hole' in Nissen or Quonset huts and our particular group called themselves 'The 13th Swipers Detachment'. We had to steal 'coke' from the coke yard to keep our one and only stove going in order to keep ourselves warm, and even then the fire would go out at night and the barracks were always cold in the morning. We also made moonlight requisitions of other essentials which we felt we needed to survive the ordeal. Cold showers in February, whilst standing in four inches of cold water were normal, and quite invigorating to say the least. Sanitary conditions were very trying. Water had to be carried in buckets to be used in our huts for washing and the British were still using 'Honey Buckets' for toilet facili-

ties. The passes to Nottingham made things look a lot better. Nottingham was also a friendly city and gave the Yanks a wonderful reception. I spent a lot of time writing letters home, often to help pass the time. This created problems part of the time, because if you were found in the barracks at night and they needed someone for KP duty the next day, you were it! It didn't take long to learn the tricks and start making the trip to Nottingham to stay out of the way of 1st Sergeant Frank M. Smith.

If the British approach to life bewildered the Americans the reverse was also true. The stereotypical no-nonsense 'Yank' way of doing things was viewed with amusement and admiration by those who worked in close proximity to them. Whereas RAF station commanders at Bottesford were expected to live in quarters next to the Officers' Mess, the American Colonel's first order on arrival was to have his bed moved into his office in the headquarters. Bob Williamson witnessed another example:

After a heavy snowfall the cables used by the Direction Finding Station to key our transmitters became unserviceable, but we were able to communicate with them by telephone. Such a breakdown was critical because the DF station played an important partin the success of our bomber missions. The 'lines' as we knew them came under the jurisdiction of the Post Office engineers, but after 24 hours they were still unserviceable, so we called upon the Americans for assistance. Boy, did they move! Out came the maps and then a big lumbering vehicle appeared with a large coil of wire mounted on a drum. Off it went through the snow in a direct line towards the DF station, and within a few minutes another vehicle turned up requesting a 'Limey' engineer to hook up the wires at the other end. We were just in time to see the cable laying vehicle charging through some poor farmer's gate that was too narrow to let it through. OB1 was rapidly back on air, but within minutes there were repercussions from the farmer whose gate had disappeared... After a brief interview with an American officer the farmer disappeared, so no doubt he was well compensated!

The Baggaley family worked Beck Farm opposite the HF transmitting station, whose RAF crew charged the 2 volt accumulator for their radio and swapped 120v batteries for butter, eggs and homemade bread. Their youngest son, Maurice, attended the school in Long Bennington and, like the rest of the family, had a pass to allow him through the American checkpoint on Sewstern Lane. It was an exciting time for a young boy. One afternoon he was amazed to see a Piper L-4 spotter plane executing a 'touch and go' ahead of him on the lane, and along with other local children who constantly pestered the Americans for chewing gum, he was sometimes allowed into the camp cinema to watch cartoons. Local legend in Bottesford has it that the village stocks were stolen one night by practical jokers. After much protest they mysteriously reappeared, and although no-one ever admitted to it, the roar of a jeep in the dead of night aroused strong suspicions! But even harmless fun sometimes ended in tragedy. Motor transport for visits into Nottingham was plentiful, but the blackout, frequent fog and unfamiliarity with winding country lanes were a real hazard to driving. Because of the problems the Americans often drove their vehicles in convoys, and one night when such a convoy was returning from a dance in Melton, the lead driver lost control on a bend just outside Bottesford. Norah Meglio, formerly Norah Turgoose of Sherwood but now living in New York wrote:

After discharge from the WAAFs following the death of my mother I met my American Air Force husband at the Palais de Danse. I was actually in the second lorry which crashed into the first when it missed a bend in the road and struck a tree. All of the occupants were thrown clear of the vehicles and strewn about the field. The driver of the first lorry was killed and several others were injured. I suffered a broken arm but don't remember too much else as I was knocked unconscious and woke up in the hospital hours later. The medics had no arm splints due to a shortage, so I was sent home with a leg splint the next morning.

The 436th Troop Carrier Group's brief time at Bottesford was drawing to a close and in early March the group moved to station 486, Membury, where they now came under the control of the 53rd TCW. The 436th's replacement, the 440th TCG (comprising the 95th, 96th, 97th and 98th Troop Carrier Squadrons) began arriving by air on March 11th, although the Group Commander, Lieutenant Colonel Frank X. Krebs did not formally took command of the station until the 23rd. Like their predecessors, the Group's aircraft had flown in from the United States. The long flight over the Atlantic caused some difficulties for Lieutenant John Lottimer of the 97th Troop Carrier Squadron, who missed his landfall in Cornwall and was forced to crash-land in Southern Ireland with no fuel. As usual, the Irish demonstrated their lop-sided neutrality and, rather than interning the crew, secretly drove them to Belfast in unmarked Army cars. There is no record of what the 440th TCG made of Bottesford, but by late March the worst of the winter weather was over and the onset of spring made the surroundings appear far better. The bicycles which had originally resulted in bruises and plaster casts, now came into their own for exploring the countryside. PFC Wally Weinkam of the 50th TCW recalled:

I usually walked to Bottesford because our G.I. bicycles were very heavy and crude. One day an English gentleman stopped and rode me to Bottesford. He gave me his card and invited me to visit him at his home. He was David Lochtie of Beechwood, Bottesford, and his wife's name was Elizabeth. I spent a number of enjoyable evenings at their house, and on one occasion Elizabeth gave me two eggs. I returned to our hut about midnight and woke up my buddies, Frank Ehrman, Clayton Hesser, Raymond Seaton, Walt Pettit, Julius Meister and Norstein. Norstein crabbed me for waking him up, but we fried the two eggs and the six of us shared them. They were the first fresh eggs any of us had tasted since leaving the U.S.A. — one cannot imagine how delicious they were! The Lochties were very nice to me. David was an executive from a firm in London and had been sent to the Midlands to escape the bombing. He was instrumental in allowing me to purchase a Raleigh bicycle from a

Hut companions of the Headquarters, 50th Troop Carrier Wing, Bottesford 1944. Left to right: Wally Weinkam, Raymond Seaton, Eugene Norstein, Walt F. Pettit, Clayton Hesser, Frank Ehrman and Julius Meister. (F. Ehrman)

shop in the village, and me and Walt Pettit did considerable cycling around the country. One day on the road to Belvoir Castle we stopped to talk to an attractive lady walking her dogs. It happened to be the Duchess of Rutland. She was living in the gatehouse at the time because the house was too costly to heat, and said she grew flowers to help pay the bills.

During a training flight on March 30th a 97th Troop Carrier Squadron C-47 flown by Lieutenant Locke suffered a fire in the port engine. Locke and his crew were unable to extinguish the flames and were at far too low an altitude to bale out, so he hurriedly looked for a suitable a spot for a forced landing. He chose a site at Derby near an Army ordnance depot. As Locke had hoped, the soldiers saw the plane come down and rushed to his assistance. They were quickly able to put out the flames, and Lieutenant Locke was praised for his cool thinking as was Lieutenant Roznek who had first spotted the fire.

April was an extremely busy month for training. On the night of the 6th the 440th practised assembling in darkness and getting into loose formation.

As Bomber Command had found over the past few years, to have hundreds of aircraft milling around in the night skies was extremely dangerous, given the risk of collision: to do so in formation was a new and far riskier departure. The other obstacle was navigating over a blacked-out landscape, but these were crucial skills for the troop carrier crews to master, given that on D-Day paratroopers and equipment would have to be dropped close to their objectives to stand any chance of success. For this reason there was a flurry of practice drops as the month progressed, mostly with the 82nd Airborne Division camped around Leicester. On the 11th there was Operation 'Payload', involving the 456th Parachute Field Artillery Battalion; on the 13th it was the turn of the 507th Parachute Infantry Regiment to be dropped for Operation 'Pitch'. Operation 'Faithful' on April 18th again involved elements of the 82nd Airborne Division, and yet another practice mission involving the 82nd coded 'Playball' was followed by 'Hopeful' on the 24th. However, practice could not continue for ever, and like every other unit about to take part in the invasion it was time for the 440th to take up position closer to the south coast. On April 26th officers and men of the 440th TCG and the 50th Troop Carrier Wing departed for Exeter. The 50th's Wing historical report observed that the determination was now there to 'Git thar fustest with the mostest'. Assembling with the 50th on southern airfields were its sister units, the 52nd and 53rd Troop Carrier Wings. Between them they now administered fifteen Troop Carrier Groups, each one comprised of four Troop Carrier Squadrons. In turn each of the four squadrons had a paper strength of sixteen C-47's, meaning that there were roughly 960 transport aircraft available for the invasion.

Although there were now no flying units in residence, Bottesford was still in American hands as a storage area for gliders. A detachment from Snailwell's 33rd Mobile Repair and Reclamation Squadron had arrived at the aerodrome in early June to inspect and repair gliders, but by the time that D-Day approached Bottesford had taken on a new function. Ron Shaw wrote:

When the invasion was approaching the hangars were filled with dozens of hospital beds and I was told that I'd be given some men, we'd be armed, and we were just going to be available to go over to the battlefront to make ourselves useful, guard prisoners, help with equipment, anything at all. But no casualties ever came to Bottesford and the beds disappeared within a very few weeks. They'd expected terrific amounts of wounded, but fortunately they just didn't happen.

The D-Day experiences of the two former Bottesford units, the 436th and 440th Troop Carrier Groups bear out Ron Shaw's comments. The 436th dropped 1,084 paratroopers and twelve artillery guns over Normandy on the morning of June 6th without loss to itself. The 440th at Exeter lost three C-47's on D-Day and three more on a re-supply mission the following day. Although total invasion casualties were heavy, they were by no means as heavy as initially feared.

CHAPTER SEVENTEEN

'Heavies'

In the three weeks since allied forces had gained their toe-hold in Normandy the Germans had fought back fiercely but were unable to prevent the push inland. The airborne troops who had begun the assault in the early hours of June 6th were now fighting as infantry in the dense bocage, and the gliders which for many months had crowded Bottesford's hangars and landing ground were amongst the thousands littering the fifty square miles of American drop zones around the base of the Cherbourg peninsula. The urgent need to store gliders had now ended and the closeness of the southern aerodromes to the battlefront made them a better choice for staging the mammoth airborne supply operation needed to continue the offensive. In July the IXth AAF therefore vacated Fulbeck, Balderton, Langar and Bottesford in favour of more suitable aerodromes in the south-west, although Barkston Heath, Cottesmore, Saltby and Folkingham were retained. Within two months Langar and Fulbeck were temporarily back under American control for 'Operation Market-Garden', but Bottesford was destined to remain in RAF hands until its closure.

In the two years since 207 Squadron's residency the training of aircrews had come a long way. In October 1942 the conversion flights on all bomber squadrons were amalgamated to form separate 'Heavy Conversion Units'. Crews now graduated from medium bombers at Operational Training Units to Heavy Conversion Units, and then having familiarised themselves with the peculiarities of 'heavies', were posted on to their squadrons. But although this removed the burden from operational squadrons, it was by no means perfect. Although there were plenty of Halifaxes and Stirlings to spare for training, the lack of Lancasters meant that those intended for Lancaster squadrons would have to attend both an HCU, and then a familiarisation course at a Lancaster Finishing School before becoming operational. The result was that Lancaster crews took longer to train than any others, but by July 1944 a few Lancasters could at last be spared. 5 Group's 1668 Heavy Conversion Unit about to be re-formed at Bottesford would be the first to train its crews from start to finish solely on Lancasters. The post of Chief Flying Instructor went to Wing Commander B.R.W. Hallows, formerly CFI at Winthorpe. 'Darky' Hallows had joined the RAFVR in 1938. In April 1942 whilst with 97 Squadron, he took part in the famous daylight low-level raid on the M.A.N. factory in Augsburg. Seven of the twelve raiders were shot down, but the remainder pressed on doggedly. Squadron Leader Nettleton of 44 Squadron received the VC for leading the raid, and Brian Hallows was awarded the DFC. He wrote:

Mine was a fairly unique job, and the Lancaster HCU meant that it cut two months at least off a crew's total training, in that, after the Stirling or Halifax HCU, they did not then have to go on a Lancaster conversion course (as had been the case before). The basic set-up was for two flights (really squadrons) engaged in flying, and a ground training flight. This eventually expanded to three flying squadrons. The crews came to us as pilot, navigator, flight engineer, bomb aimer/front gunner, wireless operator and rear gunner — six in all. We added another gunner for the mid-upper turret, making a crew of seven. The pilot and flight engineer first learned to fly the Lancaster, with the other crew members training on the ground in their specialist roles — navigation, radar signals, gunnery and bomb aiming.

Initially we had to set everything up from scratch, and the ground training side in particular caused many headaches. We had to 'acquire' all the facilities for every aspect of training. This required dummy front, rear and mid-upper turrets, as well as a complete dummy fuselage for flight engineering and other training. When the pilot, flight engineer and navigator were ready, the whole crew set off on 'Bullseyes' which involved several hours flying, bombing and gunnery practice on live ranges. Flying was by both day and night, and they got 50-75 hours in their time with us.

As the HCU's personnel began to arrive there were still a few Americans on the station, and the RAF gratefully ate American rations until their own cooking facilities were set up. In the meantime a survey of aerodrome buildings showed many to need repair and redecoration. Doors and floorboards had been removed and burned to stave off the miserable English weather, and on two sites the damage was so great that they were temporarily abandoned. An investigation was made by officers of the USAAF Ninth Troop Carrier Command Substitution Unit and repairs were begun immediately. The task was not made easier by the scarcity of tools, and most of the men, fresh from operational squadrons, viewed the work with little enthusiasm. One such airman was 20-year-old Corporal James Paxton, a Fitter/Armourer who had joined up a month before war broke out:

All my service since passing out from Halton had been on either operational squadrons or on operational stations, and quite frankly I was none too pleased with my posting to a training unit. In common with many of my fellows in the armaments trades, I regarded it as something of a come-down. From the early days, pre-aircraft times, we were beginning to build up a little in numbers and were at that time under the direction of the station admin. officer and station warrant officer, as were several other NCO's including two sergeants, class 'E' reservists. On working parade one day we were informed that we were to be sorted out according to trades with a view to employing us appropriately. The two sergeants in question had great difficulty keeping straight faces. On dismissal, one with whom I'd been working passed the comment, 'This should be interesting — I'm a rigger, rigid dirigibles. Bring me a rigid dirigible and I'll rig it for you!'. On hearing that, the other old boy remarked that he was a Fitter, Gnome Rotary engines, but that he hadn't seen any around for quite a while! Such were the founder members of 1668!

Gradually, more men and equipment began to arrive and the various sections took shape. Whilst the instructors laboured on putting together a ground and flying training syllabus, the Engineering Officer, Wing Commander King, took stock of the maintenance situation. The paper strength of 1668 was 36 Lancasters, but since front-line squadrons had first priority it had to make do with whatever was left, namely a variety of aged Mk I's, II's and III's. Given the varied marks engine fitters had to cope with Rolls-Royce Merlin XX's, XXII's, XXIV's, XXVIII's, XXXVIII's, and in the case of the Lancaster II's, with Bristol Hercules Mks VI and XVI! It was virtually impossible to stock enough spares to carry out servicing, and since all of the aircraft were 'ex-ops', many were nearing the end of their useful lives. When Group had trawled front-line units for spare aircraft it had duly received the ropiest examples imaginable, and eight of the first batch delivered were all within fifty hours of their major inspection!

With such trials to endure 'Wingco' King ran a tight ship. It was his boast that since he'd held every rank from Aircraftman 2nd Class to Wing Commander, no ploy could fool him when it came to skiving because he'd tried them all himself! James Paxton remembers a Lancaster which seemed particularly prone to magneto'drop' on the port inner engine. It was intermittent, inconsistent, and had defied all the experts. A recently arrived junior engineering officer ordered a corporal engine fitter to check the oil filters, but instead the corporal took out a torch and began to examine the ground in the vicinity of the port wheel. At this point Wing Commander King arrived, and the junior officer anxiously asked the NCO what he thought he was doing. 'I'm looking for your bloody mag. drop' he replied, 'I've just as much chance of finding it here as in the oil filters!'. Rather than put the man on a charge, 'Kingy' asked for a torch himself — to help in the search!

The presence of the Hercules engined Lancaster Mk II's is worthy of note, because only 300 of this sub-type were built out of total Lancaster production run of 7,377. Since the supply of Hercules engines were plentiful the conversion to the powerful radials had been made in the hope of reducing demands on Rolls-Royce. However, when the American Packhard company began to produce Merlins under licence orders for more Mk II's were cancelled. Operational losses meant that the 300 produced quickly became depleted, and so the remainder were relegated to training duties, being used by 1668 HCU for familiarisation. Until finally struck off charge in March 1945, Bottesford was to receive almost all of the survivors. Coincidentally, since the crews under training had mostly flown Hercules engined Wellingtons at OTU, they found the transition onto Lancasters much easier. Their enthusiasm was not shared by the staff training pilots, only one of whom had experience of the type, so that in the final days before courses began they were forced to fly in pairs to gain air time! After frantic scrounging by the engineering staff, it was the second week of September 1944 before the ten crews of No.1 Course finally began the flying stage of their instruction, having spent the first week on ground school. However, many of the aircraft had still not arrived and the ground facilities required further work, for which reason No.2 course had to be delayed. The difficulties were compounded by a lack of chocks, towing arms and engine inspection trestles. There were as yet no spares in the stores and only four jacks on the entire station! Throughout the next few months 1668's Lancasters were plagued with electrical faults brought about by dampness.

Due to a re-organisation in RAF training on November 1st the station came under the control of the newly formed 7 Group (Training) Bomber Command based at St. Vincent's, Grantham. A new teleprinter line was installed by G.P.O. engineers but, more significantly, in line with current policy Bottesford and Langar found themselves linked together to form a single administrative unit — No.72 Base. In a subsequent re-shuffle Group Captain Flinn took over command of 72 Base, and Group Captain Ken Batchelor DFC was posted in as Bottesford's new station CO. Other changes included the re-location of the station headquarters and the arrival of the 7 Group Communications flight, bringing with it more aircraft and more headaches for the overworked engineering staff. Langar now also housed an HCU, No. 1669 operating Halifaxes. From this point on visiting 'Halibags' would often 'lob in', but on November 25th 1944 one of 1669's aircraft was forced to make a night emergency landing, colliding with a hut on one of the dispersals, fortunately unoccupied at the time. This type of visitor the station could well do without!

Before long the winter fogs made the flying side of the courses fall weeks behind the ground instruction. Bottesford had always suffered from poor visibility and ground mist, not helped by the smoke from Nottingham's factories. With the number of trainees increasing rapidly, the facilities were stretched to breaking point. The cramped night flying billets in particular became filled to capacity, so much so,that as one former 'inmate' observed, it was a wonder anyone slept at all with the chorus of snoring and other unpleasant noises and odours! In each hut, 'duty crews' were detailed to monitor the weather every morning and to inform their colleagues as to the suitability of conditions for flying. Sergeant Don Moore, a flight engineer U/T at Bottesford in late 1944 recalled a Canadian crew who, on looking out of the window one morning shouted gleefully 'Flying's off! Can't see outside!'. Everybody settled back down again, but their slumbers were soon interrupted by an irate instructor. Outside it was in fact a bright, sunny day, and the 'fog' nothing more than condensation on the windows. As a penance, the occupants of the hut were made to run around the perimeter track.

The winter of 1944/45 must have been an unusually miserable one, even by Bottesford's standards. By December there were 2,373 members of the RAF and 462 WAAFs on the station, almost 3,000 in all. Wing Commander Hallows returned in November following an operation only to be diagnosed as having jaundice. He spent Christmas in the SSQ on a diet which, he recalls, did nothing to raise his spirits! For others on the station there were well attended dances and parties, for despite the recent bloody nose at Arnhem and a German counter attack in the Ardennes within the last few days, all were aware that this would surely be the last Christmas of the war.

'Char and a Wad' — the all important Y.M.C.A. tea waggon and its civilian volunteer staff outside the garage on the Old Communal Site, 1945. (R. Williamson)

In the meantime, Ken Batchelor was posted on to command Mildenhall, Charles Flinn reverted back to CO of Bottesford and Air Commodore J.W.F. Merer came from Syerston to take over 72 Base. In January it was also time for 'Darky' Hallows to move on, taking over 627 Squadron at Woodhall Spa. With illness and a blizzard of paperwork, he had only managed a few hours flying in his four months as CFI and gratefully handed over to Wing Commander W.N. Crebbin, who was to remain with the HCU until its disbandment.

For the officers at least, life was brightened up by the monthly mess parties, for which each gave a day's pay. Guests included members of the ATS from a nearby depot, and nurses from the Nottingham City Hospital, both groups reciprocating by inviting the officers to their dances. Officers were also attended parties held at the RASC depot in Bottesford village. For the airmen and women the Entertainments Officer had gathered together the more talented members of the station to form the 'Bottesfordians', a concert party which played to packed houses on camp and toured the district. Bob Williamson particularly remembered an airman named Aubrey Mirrelson who impersonated George Formby. He also recalled a visit by 'Prima Scala and his Accordian Band'. Having befriended an Italian P.O.W. named Mario from the camp in the nearby village of Allington, Bob arranged for him to meet Prima Scala before the concert. He had always thought the latter something of a fraud, but his suspicions were disproved when the maestro and Mario began to chat away in Italian!

Back in December a station lending library had been opened, with a complement of 950 books which could be borrowed for the princely sum of 1d for two books for two weeks. With a view to the needs of a postwar world, education and training classes were also started in earnest, with four airmen learning about building construction on day release in Newark, whilst others enrolled on correspondence courses or began evening classes at University College, Nottingham. For WAAFs classes in domestic science and mothercraft were deemed to be more suitable, completely ignoring the skills they had trained in over the past few years and showing that although for some it was to be a 'brave new world', for others things were expected to remain as they were. A news room was also opened, and the station music circle concentrated on the works of Beethoven. For the more energetic a hangar was equipped with facilities for badminton, netball, skittle ball and six-a-side hockey and football, and on three nights a week there was an inter-section table tennis tournament! Outside, waterlogged fields led to the postponement of many sporting fixtures. However, as James Paxton relates, entertainment was inadvertently provided for 'erks' one day on parade:

The whole unit was paraded one bright, sunny morning before Group Captain Flinn. We were drawn up into a hollow square for inspection, with the ritual checking of people for haircuts and suchlike. On inspecting the front rank of the maintenance flight, the CO stopped in front of a corporal, looked hard at him, raised his eyebrows, and glanced at the officer in charge of this section of the parade. The officer promptly turned on his heel and told the SWO to take the corporal's name and number as he needed a haircut. At this point, before the SWO could react, the corporal broke ranks, stepping one pace forward in the correct manner (at this point you could have heard a pin drop), and asked, 'Haircut? Who, me sir?'. Then without waiting for a reply, with his right hand he removed his forage cap, and with his left hand he removed his wig to reveal a gleaming scalp, saying as he did so, 'Certainly sir. Will this do, sir?'. The incident was all the more amusing for the fact that the officer who had given the order, a Wing Commander flying, had hair so long that it practically covered his greatcoat collar! Group Captain Flinn could hardly keep a straight face, and immediately dismissed the parade. The 'hairless' corporal had a bright red wig, supplied by the service when his own hair was lost due to enemy action. He could often be seen in the maintenance hangar, wig askew, scratching his head as he puzzled out some technical problem.

January 1945 brought no improvement in weather. Snow, ice, fog and low cloud meant that flying was scrubbed for days on end, or as in December, exercises cancelled half way through. Such periods at least gave time for repair work about the station. Three of the older hangars defied all attempts to make them waterproof and half of the perimeter track had to be re-concreted due to the reappearance of cracks. The only ray of hope was the reopening of 5 Site after redecoration. On the last Sunday of the month the

Bishop of Leicester also consecrated the new station church. At the same time, moves were made to beautify the area by planting conifers around the station. In the meantime an increasing backlog of trainees meant that 4 Site was forced to re-open, and a sudden thaw brought a plague of burst water pipes!

In the late afternoon of Monday 15th January the weather cleared sufficiently to allow flying. At 2030 hours Lancaster LM619, engaged in a light bombing exercise, crashed and exploded at Westborough, about half a mile from Long Bennington. Only the rear gunner, Sergeant Ashby, survived. In such circumstances it was often difficult to establish a cause. Although a Court of Enquiry attributed the crash to a loss of control in haze following an overshoot, with the combination of poor weather, war-weary aircraft and inexperienced crews such accidents were inevitable. As at all airfields, bird strikes were another constant hazard. On 26th February Pilot Officer Petfield was taking off when a flock flew across his path, smashing through the perspex and damaging a propeller blade. With so many experienced aircrew as instructors complacency could also be equally dangerous. Thirty-five year-old Flying Officer Harold Brightwell had been a chartered surveyor before the war, and was finally accepted for aircrew in 1942. In October 1944 he found himself posted to Bottesford as a navigational instructor, and he has particular cause to remember two unusual trainees:

A few days ago I had to refer to my logbook and was reminded of the advent of two Chinese captains who arrived at Bottesford in early '45 to become better acquainted with Lancs. Naturally, they were the centre of much curiosity, and were known as captains 'Bang-On' and 'Press-On'. One real name was Chen, but I cannot recall the other. Their command of the English language was minimal, but their capacity for ale was never plumbed — we gave up long before! At about the same time an experienced PFF bomb aimer named 'Stew' persuaded me to teach him the rudiments of navigation. When it was time for the Chinese solo flight I went along with Stew, he insisting on navigating. After persuading 'Bang-On' that it was usual to close the bomb doors before take-off, we were airborne. I got Stew settled and then retired to the rest bed with a book. I eventually fell asleep, only to be rudely awakened by Stew saying that he was lost. I looked outside, and like the Ancient Mariner, there was water, water, everywhere. I had no charts and Stew's were incomprehensible, so the only thing to do was to fly on the reciprocal course until we struck land, and then attempt to map read back to base. Mission accomplished, I was very glad to be back on terra firma!

But even the presence of an instructor did not guarantee safety. On February 7th Flying Officer Walker, demonstrating three engined overshoots to Flying Officer Wilkinson in JA684, crashed just beyond the threshold of the runway. The aircraft was burnt out and three crew members admitted to hospital. In another professionally embarrassing episode, the Station Fire Officer fell into an inspection pit at Langar and broke his leg!

CHAPTER EIGHTEEN

It's a lovely day tomorrow...

By March 1945 the allies were rapidly advancing into Germany but, despite chronic shortages of fuel and other necessities, German resistance continued to be fierce. With insufficient resources to prevent RAF bombers reaching their targets, the Luftwaffe was forced to turn to night intruder operations over Britain in an attempt to catch the returning bombers at their most vulnerable, whilst over their bases. The first attack took place on the night of March 3/4th when around 70 German nightfighters roamed eastern Britain from Northumberland to Oxfordshire. The success of the attack led to others, although on a much smaller scale. On the night of Monday March 20th Junkers 88s and 188s mingled with RAF Mosquitoes returning from a raid on Berlin, avoiding radar detection. Flying Officer John Johns, a 24-year-old West Countryman undergoing pilot training, was flying with his crew and an instructor that night. The time was eight-thirty.

I had just landed the aircraft and was still on the runway when all lights were extinguished. There was just enough light to see the perimeter track, onto which I turned right. To my surprise the intruder attacked, shooting up the left side of the track. Before he returned I shot into an empty dispersal, switched off, and hurried to a shelter — the crew beat me by yards! The following day we had to comb the airfield for 'butterfly bombs'. Once landed they became 'live' and could do nasty damage if disturbed. So all the station personnel were lined up and meticulously searched the whole airfield in a series of controlled sweeps. If any foreign object was spotted, up went a hand — the line stopped — and the bomb disposal boys moved in. The exercise took all day and involved everyone, apart from a few cooks and communications staff. The following day, special teams had to examine all buildings, gutters and other such points. This went on for several days.'

The lone German had crossed the aerodrome twice, strafing as he went and dropping several small anti-personnel bombs close to the communal site. Miraculously, the only casualties were a Lancaster parked on its dispersal and several pieces of crockery in the Mess. In the process Bottesford had the distinction of suffering the very last German bombing raid of the war against Britain, ironic considering how for two years the airfield's Manchesters and Lancasters had been engaged in meting out destruction across Germany.

Such interruptions aside, March also saw a new record of 2263 hours flying completed from the airfield. Again, the increased volume of traffic was causing heavy wear to the perimeter track, and newly delivered Bristol

A blackened scene of utter devastation — Cologne from the air, 1945. Photo taken from a 1668 Lancaster on a 'Cook's Tour' of Germany in the first days of the peace. (F. Fazackerley)

Beaufighters intended for nightfighter affiliation could not use the main runway due to its poor state of repair. On the plus side, after three years the dispersed sites were finally connected up to a proper sewage system. The second highlight of the month was the Harrison Cup final football match. In its first (and last) season, Bottesford came runner-up to the champions, Swinderby.

With the capitulation of Germany on May 8th 1945 there was a feeling of anti-climax across the station. Just a few weeks before, Marshal of the Royal Air Force Lord Trenchard had visited Bottesford to address personnel on the need for patience in awaiting their discharges. Nevertheless, after six years of struggle, when the end of the war in Europe came, it still came as a shock. Although there was a well-attended celebration dance in the evening, many people seemed to prefer to spend the day's stand-down in quiet reflection. The day after it was back to work again...

Throughout the war the groundstaff had worked tirelessly to ensure that the aircraft were kept serviceable. Their contribution was rewarded after V.E. day by cramming them into Lancasters and taking them on 'Cooks Tours' of Germany to see the destruction their work had helped to achieve. The scenes of utter devastation made a strong impression, at least enough to temporarily forget airsickness and take out previously forbidden cameras and snap a few souvenir photos. But despite the levity the work was not over yet. Japan had still to be beaten and the trainees learned that their services might well be required in the Far East. Nevertheless, thoughts were very much towards the future, and at Bottesford, as elsewhere, there was a spate of marriages. 1668's Squadron Leader Barns married a local farmer's daughter at Grantham with Flight Lieutenant Hamilton of the gunnery section as best man. A Glaswegian, Bill Hamilton, had flown from Bottesford in 1942 with 207 Squadron, and following a second tour found himself posted back as an instructor. He and his wife Evelyn rented a house from the Burrows family in the Nook, and it was here that Bill's first son was born. As already mentioned, Allington was now home to an Italian prisoner of war camp. Italy had capitulated in September 1943, and the men, mostly conscripts captured in the western desert, were allowed to work for local farmers or around the aerodrome and army camp. As well as cutting a swathe through the female population they were also employed by officers as batmen. Bill Hamilton's batman cycled daily to their house where he cooked, cleaned, and spoilt their baby terribly!

On fine evenings Group Captain Flinn liked to play golf with other officers. For those preferring a night on the town the LNER was as much a lifeline as ever, but there were increasing problems with airmen using the late night Nottingham-Grantham train. They regularly pulled the communication cord before the train reached the station, making their escape across the fields to avoid Service Police waiting to check passes. After several such incidents drivers began to ignore the brake and drag their trains into the station. Even more brazen airmen would hand the ticket inspector a bus ticket, cinema ticket — anything they had in their pockets! The station master, incensed at such blatant disregard for his authority, sent a bag of tickets to the station headquarters with the request that something be done. Ron Shaw was intrigued to see a WAAF carefully going through the bag and asked her what she was doing, 'Seeing which ones I can use again', she replied innocently.

By the time that Group Captain J.H.T. Simpson DSO took over the station in July, Langar was on 'care and maintenance' and training at Bottesford had slowed almost to a stop. It had already been decided to close the station and transfer 1668 HCU to pre-war Cottesmore, a move hastened by renewed subsidence on the main runway. Only 11 crews were received during July, and of the 23 who graduated that month just 8 were posted to squadrons, the rest being sent on indefinite leave. As a consequence, when harvest time came bored aircrew gladly volunteered to work for hard-pressed local farmers. In return, people like George Lovett of Normanton offered sumptuous farmhouse cooking. The meals were much sought-after, so a strict rota was drawn up to avoid fights as to who should be chosen. For three years Lovett had provided bacon to the messes, with 'something extra' prior to parties.

Quiet and forlorn, Bottesford Flying Control keeps silent watch over the deserted aerodrome. The war is over, the aircraft have departed and Bottesford relegated to use as a storage site. (H. Watson)

Rationing meant that the authorities had to be notified when pigs and cattle were to be slaughtered, but like many farmers, Lovett's pigs always seemed to have eight legs! The family were also well known because they allowed airmen to fill their haversacks with eggs, apples or pears before going on leave, always for threepence. It occurred to Bill Hamilton that it was a measly sum, and when he got to know the family betterhe asked why. 'Because', Mrs Lovett replied, 'if we'd given them to you for nothing, you wouldn't have come back!'.

On Monday August 6th 1945, in the most awesome display of the power of strategic bombing the world has ever seen, a single aircraft of the U.S. 20th Army Air Force destroyed the city of Hiroshima, and with it an estimated 80,000 people. A follow-up raid on Nagasaki three days later effectively ended the war. V.J. Day, 15th August 1945, was a day of mixed emotions at Bottesford, as it was across Britain. Very suddenly it was all over, and everyone on the station was drawn up in the recreational hangar to be addressed by Group Captain Simpson. After a short service of thanksgiving by the padre, everyone was dismissed to celebrate the day as they wished. The engineering section were taking no chances, and removed the contact breakers from all aircraft to discourage joy-riders. Exactly a month later on September 15th, Battle of Britain Day, motor transport provided by 7 Group began ferrying 1668 HCU personnel to Cottesmore. The thirty or so aircraft on strength were also flown out that same day and Bottesford officially closed to flying on the 17th, almost exactly four years to the day after it had opened.

Shortly after 1668 HCU had departed Bottesford became a sub-site of 256 Maintenance Unit based at Barkston Heath, responsible for the storage and disposal of surplus equipment. With no further need for material, the runways and taxiways rapidly filled up with lines and lines of vehicles, factory-fresh but awaiting disposal. Elsewhere the living sites were crammed with mattresses and bedding, and what couldn't be stored was either sold off to locals 'for a few bob' or unceremoniously burnt. It was a sad end to an illustrious career.

Although RAF Bottesford officially closed in 1948 with most of the landing ground coming under the plough, it still had one more job to fulfil — as a store for some of the millions of tonnes of wartime ammunition stockpiles still awaiting disposal. Hundreds of bombs were stacked along the runways, behind the B1 hangar across the Normanton road and on the grass verges beside it. When the bomb dump was finally cleared in the 1960s the pyrotechnics remaining gave local children a firework display they would remember for years to come! John Rose from nearby Kilvington had been farming the airfield since just after the war, and after the Air Ministry auctioned it off in lots in 1954 he gradually acquired piece after piece until eight years later he owned the whole of the former technical site and landing ground. With remarkable foresight he realised that with its ten hangars, the airfield had potential for industrial storage, and set up the Newark Storage Company (now a part of the Roseland Group). It is to this that the airfield owes its preservation.

Although the northern end of the main runway was torn up for hardcore in the 1970s, the perimeter track reduced in width and all the dispersals removed, the airfield today is remarkably intact. At a short service in April 1993 a commemorative plaque was placed by members of the 467/463 and 207 Squadron Associations in the refurbished control tower — now used as offices. Two years later the Aussies were back in force to plant a eucalyptus tree on the former signals square on the 50th anniversary of VE Day. For many it must inevitably have been their last pilgrimage back to England.

To the casual visitor passing through Bottesford today, the graves in the churchyard are the only reminders of a time when this quiet part of Leicestershire carried the war night after night to the heartland of Germany. Returning veterans remark on the emptiness they experience on the old 'drome. Back in 1945, those same men and women were struggling to re-adapt to civilian life. One of them was Corporal Ron Shaw, who went back again on an errand shortly after de-mob. He still returns once a year, just to remember and 'pay his respects', but his simple description of that first journey back evoke feelings that will be recognised by many of his comrades:

On Christmas Eve 1945 I went back to the aerodrome with my wife and two daughters, then aged six and ten, as I'd arranged to collect some eggs and poultry from Ablewhite's farm. We passed one of the living sites and then the Sergeants' Mess.

Bottesford from the air, looking north west, 1990. Although part of the main runway and the dispersals have long since gone, their 'ghosts' are still visible, as are the hangars and the classic 'A' shape of a wartime bomber airfield. (B. Goodwin)

One of the doors was blowing open and shut in the wind, and inside I could see pans still on the stoves. In the picket post which fronted the lane opposite Sick Quarters, a curtain fluttered in the breeze through a broken window pane. Imagine — all that activity in the war — the hustle and bustle — everything that happened there; now it was deserted, not a soul in sight...

Coming back through Normanton, past No.9 hangar, we called on an old lady and her daughter who I used to get eggs from. They'd just made mince pies in the shape of little cradles, and only a few hours before they'd had a calf born. They invited my daughters to go and have a look at it, and they were fascinated! I remember kidding them on the way home that we'd have to hurry to get back before Santa Claus! It's a memory that takes me back all those years. I could shut my eyes, and I'd be there...

Bottesford Station Commanders

Royal Air Force Station Bottesford, No. 5 (Bomber) Group

10/9/41–14/11/41	Group Captain W.G. Cheshire
15/11/41–2/3/43	Group Captain F.R.D. Swain OBE AFC
3/3/43–15/11/43	Group Captain W.N. McKechnie GC

Station 480, United States IXth Army Air Force Troop Carrier Command

18/11/43–22/3/44	Brigadier General Julian N. Chappell
23/3/44–?	Lieutenant Colonel Frank X. Krebs

Royal Air Force Station Bottesford, No.5 (Bomber) Group

1/8/44–	Group Captain C.H. Flinn

No. 72 Base, 7 Group Royal Air Force

8/11/44–1/12/44	Group Captain C.H. Flinn (Base C.O.)
8/11/44–1/12/44	Group Captain K.S. Batchelor DFC (Station C.O.)
1/12/44–?	Air Commodore J.W.F. Merer (Base C.O.)
1/12/44–10/7/45	Group Captain C.H. Flinn (Station C.O.)
4/7/45–17/9/45	Group Captain J.H.T. Simpson DSO (Station C.O.)

Bottesford Squadron/Unit Commanders

207 Squadron Royal Air Force

10/10/41–28/5/42	Wing Commander C. Fothergill
28/5/42–7/12/42	Wing Commander F.R. Jeffs AFC

90 Squadron Royal Air Force

7/11/42–6/43	Wing Commander J.C. Claydon DFC

467 Squadron Royal Australian Air Force

7/11/42–15/8/43	Wing Commander C.L. Gomm DSO DFC
15/8/43–18/8/43	Squadron Leader A.S. Raphael DFC
19/8/43–12/5/44	Wing Commander J.R. Balmer OBE

436th Troop Carrier Group, 50th Troop Carrier Wing, U.S. IXth AAF

1/4/43–1/10/45	Colonel A.N. Williams

440th Troop Carrier Group, 50th Troop Carrier Wing, U.S. IXth AAF

7/7/43–18/9/44	Lieutenant Colonel Frank X. Krebs

1668 Heavy Conversion Unit Royal Air Force

4/8/44–21/1/45	Wing Commander B.R.W. Hallows DFC
21/1/45–	Wing Commander W.N. Crebbin DFC

207 SQUADRON ROYAL AIR FORCE

23rd November 1941 — Local Flight — Manchester L7300 EM-F

P/O	A W T	Hills DFM	45304	RAF	P	Injured	
P/O		Plaistowe		RAF	2nd P	Injured	
Sgt	C	Smith	2677582	RAF	Wop/AG	Injured	
Sgt	J	van Puyenbroek	915131	RAF	Wop/AG	Injured	
F/O	S E	Pattinson	42429	RAF	Passenger	Injured	
F/O	F A	Roper	J6166	RCAF	Passenger	Injured	
P/O		Unknown					
P/O		Unknown					
Cpl		Unknown					

Both engines failed whilst on a local flight to Waddington. Crashed into Fiskerton quarry lake, 1530 hrs, from where it was later recovered by 58 Maintenance Unit.

8/9th January 1942 — Brest — Manchester L7322 EM-Q

F/O	G R	Bayley	88024	RAF(VR)	P	Killed	Crozon (Fr)
Sgt	N M	Toohill	A404786	RAAF	2nd P	Killed	NKG
Sgt	A G	Harris	920869	RAF(VR)	Obs	Killed	NKG
F/Sgt	J E	Jones DFM	551817	RAF	Wop/AG	Killed	NKG
Sgt	R V	Griffiths	1180830	RAF(VR)	Wop/AG	Killed	NKG
Sgt	W R	Seymour	A407808	RAAF	AG	Killed	Crozon (Fr)
Sgt	P C H	Goldie	A406450	RAAF	AG	Killed	Crozon (Fr)

Hit by flak and crashed into the sea off Crozon, France, 0600 hrs.

14/15th January 1942 — Hamburg — Manchester L7309 EM-O

P/O	G B	Dawkins DFM	114248	RAF(VR)	P	POW	
Sgt	G E	Allen	NZ404489	RNZAF	2nd P	POW	
P/O	P J	Edwards	63086	RAF(VR)	Obs	POW	
F/Sgt	J	Mercer	939719	RAF(VR)	Wop/AG	POW	
Sgt	J W	Cadman	1016939	RAF(VR)	Wop/AG	Killed	Sage (Ger)
Sgt	E G R	Bestel	R70458	RCAF	AG	POW	

Attacked by nightfighter, possibly that of Oberleutnant Rudolf Schöenert of II/NJG2. Crew abandoned aircraft which crashed near Sandel Moens, Jever, Germany at 2100 hrs.

14/15th January 1942 — Hamburg — Manchester L7523 EM-M

F/Sgt	B C	Wescombe	523056	RAF	P	Killed	Falmer (UK)
F/Sgt	F E	Thomas	1111152	RAF	2nd P	Killed	Brandesburton (UK)
Sgt	E R	Harper	92545	RAF(VR)	Obs	Killed	Wandsworth (UK)
F/Sgt	L	Sieve	902414	RAF(VR)	Wop/AG	Killed	Failsworth (UK)
Sgt	C R	Westbury	981733	RAF(VR)	Wop/AG	Killed	Nottingham (UK)
Sgt	J T	Howe	1194369	RAF(VR)	AG	Killed	Rugby(UK)
Sgt	M R	Walker	841700	RAF	AG	Killed	Wallasey (UK)

Crashed and burnt out at 2045 hrs on North Farm, Holmpton, Yorks. (now Humberside).

28th March 1942 — Training — Lancaster R5501 EM-G

Sgt	N A	Lingard	1059599	RAF(VR)	P	Killed	Worsley (UK)
Sgt	D A	Wood	1065432	RAF(VR)	2nd P	Killed	Lincoln (UK)
Sgt	R W	Cox	1251520	RAF(VR)	Obs	Killed	Mortlake (UK)
Sgt	T C	Massey	932392	RAF(VR)	Wop/AG	Killed	Camberwell (UK)

Collided with Miles Master DK973 during daylight cross-country exercise. Crashed 1320 hrs on Canwick Hill, 2 miles South of Lincoln.

8th April 1942 — **Training** — **Lancaster R5498 EM-Z**

F/Sgt	J J N	McCarthy	NZ410470	RNZAF	P	Injured	
Sgt	J D L	La Salle	R77173	RCAF	2nd P	Injured	
Sgt	J M	Leahy	982476	RAF(VR)	Obs	Injured	
Sgt	D L	Worthington	759163	RAF(VR)	Wop/AG	Injured	
Sgt	J K	Banfield	929931	RAF(VR)	Wop/AG	Injured	

Both starboard engones cut whilst on final approach, 0114 hrs. Crashed and burnt out next to Normanton Lodge.

24th May 1942 — **Training** — **Lancaster R5617 EM-T**

Sgt	T K	Paul	NZ41525	RNZAF	P	Injured	
Sgt	A P	Paterson	1378976	RAF(VR)	2nd P	Killed	Rugby (UK).
F/Sgt	R L	Mellish	R81078	RCAF	Obs	Killed	Buckland Monachorum (UK)
Sgt	C A	Pankhurst	1260384	RAF(VR)	Obs	Killed	Buckland Monachorum (UK)
Sgt	T A M	Whiteman	RAF(VR)	Wop/AG		Injured	
F/Sgt	L M	Smith	629603	RAF	Wop/AG	Killed	Newent (UK)

Crashed into Standon Hill, Tavistock, 2330 hrs, following re-call from training flight due to deteriorating weather.

3/4th June 1942 — **Bremen** — **Lancaster R5847 EM-Y**

W/O	C	Wathey	564896	RAF	P	Killed	Westerbork (NL)
Sgt	L J	Lea	748097	RAF(VR)	2nd P	Killed	Westerbork (NL)
Sgt	R R A	Jones	NZ404540	RNZAF	Obs	Killed	Westerbork (NL)
F/Sgt	T D	Atkinson	621174	RAF	Wop/AG	Killed	Westerbork (NL)
F/Sgt	T L	Musitano	1168720	RAF(VR)	Wop/AG	Killed	Westerbork (NL)
Sgt	C J M	Hall	933625	RAF(VR)	Wop/AG	Killed	Westerbork (NL)
Sgt	S G	Kerr	1118929	RAF(VR)	AG	Killed	Westerbork (NL)

Shot down by Major Gunter Radüsch of II/NJG2. Crashed 0114 hrs at Zwiggelte, 14 km SSE of Assen, Netherlands.

20/21st June 1942 — **Emden** — **Lancaster R5860 EM-Y**

F/Lt	G A	Ings	61471	RAF(VR)	P	Safe
Sgt	R	Bell-Berry	1076769	RAF(VR)	2nd P	Safe
F/Sgt	W J A	Shapter	R78148	RCAF	Obs	Safe
Sgt	J E	Bellamy		RAF	Wop/AG	Safe
Sgt	J	Culley	1186097	RAF(VR)	Wop/AG	Safe
Sgt	D R	Manser	1271941	RAF(VR)	AG	Safe
Sgt	J W E	Holland	528167	RAF	AG	Safe

Both starboard engines caught fire on the return flight. Aircraft ditched 90 miles E of Humber estuary, 0102 hrs. Crew rescued from dinghy later that morning.

5th July 1942

F/Lt	R K	Porter	82424	RAF(VR)	Died	Bottesford (UK)

11/12th July 1942 — **Danzig** — **Lancaster L7543 EM-Z**

F/Sgt	G H	Duke	1163246	RAF(VR)	P	Killed	Malbork (Pol)
F/Sgt	K H	Hart	1154131	RAF(VR)	2nd P	Killed	Malbork (Pol)
Sgt	F	Routledge	929946	RAF(VR)	Obs	Killed	Malbork (Pol)
P/O	K J	Shirley	127160	RAF	Wop/AG	Killed	Malbork (Pol)
Sgt	H A	Storey	1072974	RAF(VR)	Obs	Killed	Malbork (Pol)
F/Sgt	A P	Cullerne	924150	RAF(VR)	AG	Killed	Malbork (Pol)
F/Sgt	D A	Boldy	923995	RAF(VR)	AG	Killed	Malbork (Pol)

Believed shot down by flak in the target area.

24th July 1942 — Duisberg — Lancaster R5632 EM-N

F/Sgt	W G	Hawes	A402504	RAAF	P	Killed	NKG
Sgt	P J	Hooper	NZ404366	RNZAF	2nd P	Killed	NKG
Sgt	H F	Clarke	1183538	RAF(VR)	Obs	Killed	NKG
Sgt	E	Cartwright	1208967	RAF(VR)	Wop/AG	Killed	NKG
F/Sgt	T C	Blair	R75117	RCAF	AB	Killed	Amsterdam (NL)
F/Sgt	J C	Chiasson	R65313	RCAF	AG	Killed	NKG
Sgt	W R	Smith	1307055	RAF(VR)	AG	Killed	NKG

Believed shot crashed into the North Sea. Sgt Blair was washed ashore near Ijmuiden on October 12th.

24th July 1942 — Duisberg — Lancaster R5867 EM-T

P/O	J J N	McCarthy	NZ401470	RNZAF	P	Killed	Reichswald (Ger)
F/Sgt	J D L	La Salle	R77173	RCAF	2nd P	Killed	Reichswald (Ger)
F/Sgt	J M	Leahy	982476	RAF(VR)	Obs	Killed	Reichswald (Ger)
Sgt	D L	Worthington	759163	RAF(VR)	Wop/AG	Killed	Reichswald (Ger)
F/Sgt	R A	Edmonds	1260393	RAF(VR)	Obs	Killed	Reichswald (Ger)
F/Sgt	A	Rowland	646781	RAF(VR)	Wop/AG	Killed	Reichswald (Ger)
P/O	E L	Hayward	126810	RAF(VR)	AG	Killed	Reichswald (Ger)

Shot down at Baerl on the Dutch/German border. Crew buried at Krefeld on 28th July, reinterred at Reichswald after the war.

6th August 1942 — Training — Manchester L7385 EM-U

Sgt	A S	Pearson	1177661	RAF(VR)	P	Injured	
Sgt	J	Forbes	967145	RAF(VR)	FE	Killed	Aberdeen (UK)
Sgt	C S K	Shepherd	1112237	RAF(VR)	Wop/AG	Killed	Chester (UK)
Sgt	J	Slater	1536441	RAF(VR)	AG	Injured	
Sgt	A J C	Whitehead		RAF(VR)	AG	Injured	

In collision with Lancaster R5550 on the flarepath at 0005 hrs.

6th August 1942 — Training — Lancaster R5550 EM-B

Sgt	F S	Akerman	655412	RAF	P	Killed	Uxbridge (UK)
Sgt	H	Curson	537658	RAF	FE	Killed	Bottesford (UK)
F/Sgt	J	Brooks	924977	RAF(VR)	Obs	Killed	Arnold, Berks. (UK)
F/Sgt	A F G	Smart	1255319	RAF(VR)	Wop/AG	Injured	
F/Sgt	F R	Ikin	925453	RAF(VR)	AG	Injured	

As above.

5/6th August 1942 — Essen — Lancaster R5761 EM-T

F/Lt	G A	Ings	61471	RAF(VR)	P	Killed	Uden (NL)
Sgt	R	Bell-Berry	1076769	RAF(VR)	2nd P	Killed	Uden (NL)
W/O	W J A	Shapter	R78148	RCAF	Obs	Killed	Uden (NL)
Sgt	J	Culley	1186097	RAF(VR)	Wop/AG	Killed	Uden (NL)
F/Sgt	G C	Everitt MM	751919	RAF(VR)	Wop/AG	Killed	Uden (NL)
Sgt	D R	Manser	1271941	RAF(VR)	AG	Killed	Uden (NL)
Sgt	J W E	Holland	528167	RAF	AG	Killed	Uden (NL)

Shot down by Oberleutnant Gerhard Loos of I/NJG1. Crashed 0220 hrs at Altforst, 20 km W of Nijmegan, Netherlands.

10/11th August 1942 — Mining 'Kraut' - Kattegat — Lancaster R5499 EM-O

F/O	J G	Speir	J5136	RCAF	P	Killed	NKG
F/Sgt	L G	Cladis	1379459	RAF(VR)	2nd P	Killed	NKG
F/O	G	Easley	103574	RAF(VR)	Obs	Killed	NKG
F/O	S	Glazebrook	46019	RAF(VR)	Wop/AG	Killed	NKG
F/Sgt	M W	Atkins	R101589	RCAF	Obs	Killed	NKG
Sgt	C W	Musto	A406149	RAAF	AG	Killed	NKG
P/O	R R	Hartell	106131	RAF(VR)	AG	Killed	NKG

Presumed crashed into the sea.

12/13th August 1942 — Mainz — Lancaster R5760 EM-Y

W/O	D W	Fry	905553	RAF(VR)	P	Killed	NKG
Sgt	R W E	Holmes	629489	RAF	FE	Killed	NKG
Sgt	J W	Benn	A404881	RAAF	Obs	Killed	NKG
Sgt	S	Obard	646412	RAF	Wop/AG	Killed	NKG
Sgt	P R	Kenny	1121314	RAF(VR)	AB	Killed	NKG
Sgt	T	Fitzpatrick	1113188	RAF(VR)	Wop/AG	Killed	NKG
Sgt	H A L	Green	548497	RAF	AG	Killed	NKG

Presumed crashed into the sea.

12/13th August 1942 — Mainz — Lancaster R5633 EM-R

F/Sgt	S F	Kane	1005750	RAF(VR)	P	Killed	Durnbach (Ger)
Sgt	A I	Steel	1186364	RAF(VR)	FE	Killed	Durnbach (Ger)
W/O	B A	Brophy	R77127	RCAF	Obs	Killed	Durnbach (Ger)
Sgt	C	Racine	934271	RAF(VR)	Wop/AG	Killed	Durnbach (Ger)
Sgt	W P L	Wood	1105942	RAF(VR)	Wop/AG	Killed	Durnbach (Ger)
Sgt	D H	Whiting	1251357	RAF(VR)	Wop/AG	Killed	Durnbach (Ger)
Sgt	J	Preston	633185	RAF	AG	Killed	Durnbach (Ger)

16/17th August 1942 — Mining 'Willows' - Kiel Bay — Lancaster R5509 EM-G

F/Sgt	N J	Sutherland	NZ41631	RNZAF	P	Killed	NKG
Sgt	A M	Craig	613300	RAF	FE	Killed	NKG
Sgt	W B	McVicar	655655	RAF(VR)	Obs	Killed	NKG
Sgt	A H	McKenzie	915766	RAF(VR)	Wop/AG	Killed	NKG
Sgt	S	Spencer	131508	RAF(VR)	Wop/AG	Killed	NKG
Sgt	J	McArthur	1118847	RAF(VR)	AG	Killed	NKG
Sgt	A	Roddam	1378871	RAF(VR)	AG	Killed	NKG

Presumed crashed into the sea.

16/17th August 1942 — Mining 'Geraniums' - Kattegat — Lancaster R5616 EM-J

P/O	A J	Southwell	106144	RAF(VR)	P	Killed	Esbjerg (Den)
Sgt	J	Read	810154	RAF(VR)	FE	POW	
F/O	D J	Quinlan	J6130	RCAF	Obs	Killed	Esbjerg (Den)
F/O	W M	Edmonds	A403506	RAAF	Wop/AG	Killed	Esbjerg (Den)
Sgt	R	Robson	954712	RAF(VR)	Wop/AG	Killed	Esbjerg (Den)
Sgt	T	Douglas	632776	RAF	Wop	Killed	Esbjerg (Den)
F/Sgt	J A	McLean	R66065	RCAF	AG	Killed	Esbjerg (Den)

Crashed into the sea SSW of Mano Island, Denmark. Sgt Read was brought ashore injured.

19th August 1942 — Training — Lancaster R5863 EM-K

F/Sgt	W D	Fordwych	591266	RAF	P	Killed	Bottesford (UK)
Sgt	J C	Murphy	A401182	RAAF	2nd P	Killed	Bottesford (UK)
P/O	D V	Morris-Edwards	117479	RAF(VR)	Obs	Killed	Stoke on Trent (UK)
Sgt	S O	Spicer	1181149	RAF(VR)	Wop/AG	Killed	Hitchin (UK)
Sgt	A J	Boyne	969690	RAF(VR)	AG	Killed	Logie (UK)
Sgt	B M	Smith	1216295	RAF(VR)	AG	Killed	Carlton, Notts. (UK)

Crashed onto the road at Normanton, 0115 hrs, whilst practising three-engined overshoots.

FROM SYERSTON

27/28th August 1942 **Kassel** **Lancaster W4129 EM-R**

P/O	T D	Brown	113391	RAF(VR)	P	Killed	NKG
Sgt	E W J	Chaldecott	908544	RAF(VR)	FE	Killed	NKG
P/O	G D	Hughes	J8805	RCAF	Obs	POW	
Sgt	J	Boon	922914	RAF(VR)	Wop/AG	POW	
F/Sgt	D H	Boswell	650382	RAF	AB	POW	
Sgt	H C	Taylor	1386118	RAF(VR)	AG	Killed	NKG
F/Sgt	R A	Clement	R91302	RCAF	AG	Killed	NKG

5th September 1942 **Bremen** **Lancaster R5755 EM-N**

F/O	R G	Rowlands	A407726	RAAF	P	Killed	Hemelumer (NL)
Sgt	G	Fleck	532066	RAF(VR)	FE	Killed	NKG
P/O	A B	Hastings	120036	RAF(VR)	Obs	Killed	Lemsterland (NL)
Sgt	J C	Luton	A403411	RAAF	Wop/AG	Killed	Staveren (NL)
Sgt	F J C	Barnes	655006	RAF	Obs	Killed	Bergen (NL)
Sgt	J W	Atkinson	1105186	RAF(VR)	AG	Killed	Bergen (NL)
Sgt	C V	Pattison	778001	RAF(VR)	AG	Killed	NKG

Shot down by Unteroffizier Heinz Vinke of II/NJG2 and crashed into the Ijsselmeer E of Medemblik 0250 hrs.

9/10th September 1942 **Mining 'Silverthorn' - Kattegat** **Lancaster R5628 EM-Q**

F/Sgt	H B	Einarson	R87296	RCAF	P	Killed	NKG
Sgt	F R	Carter	1166938	RAF(VR)	FE	Killed	Lemvig (Den)
Sgt	A M	Cockie	656606	RAF(VR)	Obs	Killed	Lemvig (Den)
P/O	D W	Ross	J9288	RCAF	Wop/AG	Killed	Lemvig (Den)
Sgt	G H A	Birch	1388177	RAF(VR)	AB	Killed	NKG
Sgt	A F C	Kensett	1358378	RAF(VR)	AG	Killed	NKG
Sgt	N F	Smethurst	656871	RAF(VR)	AG	Killed	NKG

Shot down by nightfighter and crashed into the North Sea 10 km SW of Thyboron, Denmark, 0409 hrs.

16/17th September 1942 **Essen** **Lancaster L7571 QR-S**

F/Sgt	J D M	Herron	A405267	RAAF	P	POW
Sgt	R A	Strowger	640060	RAF	FE	POW
Sgt	G C	Williams	1106747	RAF(VR)	Obs	POW
Sgt	I F	Betts	1360652	RAF(VR)	Wop/AG	POW
Sgt	A R	Barnett	1100816	RAF(VR)	Wop/AG	POW
Sgt	G F	Mountney	964381	RAF(VR)	AG	POW
Sgt	J D	Nicholson	623585	RAF	AG	POW

90 SQUADRON ROYAL AIR FORCE

18th December 1942

F/Sgt	I M J	McGavin MiD	561820	RAF	Killed	Hamble (UK).

Killed when the undercarriage collapsed on the Stirling he was repairing.

467 SQUADRON ROYAL AUSTRALIAN AIR FORCE

21st December 1942 **Munich** **Lancaster W4191 EM-Q**

F/O	D G	Bannerman	NZ414380	RNZAF	2nd P	Killed	Oud Leusden (NL)

Killed flying with a 207 Squadron crew from Langar.

8/9th January 1943			**Duisberg**			**Lancaster ED367 PO-H**	
Sgt	A M	Wark	J16662	RCAF	P	Killed	NKG
Sgt	E J C	Florey	577867	RAF	FE	Killed	NKG
F/Sgt	D H B	Powell	R82995	RCAF	Nav	Killed	NKG
F/Sgt	S V	Woyce	R93302	RCAF	Wop	Killed	NKG
Sgt	R T	Hanbridge	J16661	RCAF	AB	Killed	NKG
F/Sgt	H A	Horton	R135101	RCAF	AG	Killed	NKG
Sgt	J W	Humphries	1236942	RAF(VR)	AG	Killed	NKG

Presumed crashed into the sea.

16/17th January 1943			**Berlin**			**Lancaster ED360 PO-D**	
F/Sgt	A J	Broemeling	R121904	RCAF	AG	Killed	Long Bennington (UK)

Died of anoxia.

17/18th January 1943			**Berlin**			**Lancaster W4378 PO-N**	
Sgt	K R	Aicken	NZ414372	RNZAF	P	Killed	NKG
Sgt	W J	Carter	577959	RAF	FE	Killed	NKG
F/O	T O	Truscott	125301	RAF(VR)	Nav	Killed	NKG
Sgt	F	Hanson	1114059	RAF(VR)	Wop	Killed	NKG
Sgt	C S H	Morley	711065	RAF(VR)	AB	Killed	NKG
Sgt	F	Logie	778801	RAF(VR)	AG	Killed	NKG
Sgt	A P	Smith	1265587	RAF(VR)	AG	Killed	NKG

Presumed crashed into the sea.

19/20th February 1943			**Wilhelmshaven**			**Lancaster ED525 PO-**	
F/Lt	J B	Michie	78731	RAF(VR)	P	Killed	NKG
Sgt	R	Bailey	1104712	RAF(VR)	FE	Killed	NKG
F/O	W K	Komaiko	J11218	RCAF	Nav	Killed	NKG
Sgt	G	McLoughlin	1076873	RAF(VR)	Wop	Killed	NKG
Sgt	J S	Turner	1267135	RAF(VR)	AB	Killed	NKG
Sgt	R A J	King	1601208	RAF(VR)	AG	Killed	NKG
F/Sgt	H L	Brown	R1252249	RCAF	AG	Killed	NKG

Presumed crashed into the sea.

19/20th February 1943			**Wilhelmshaven**			**Lancaster ED529 PO-**	
Sgt	H B	Vine	1378781	RAF(VR)	P	Killed	NKG
Sgt	R	Sinden	577701	RAF	FE	Killed	NKG
Sgt	K	Westthorp	1046328	RAF(VR)	Nav	Killed	NKG
Sgt	D A	Booth	1378781	RAF(VR)	Wop	Killed	NKG
Sgt	J	McKee	1089032	RAF(VR)	AB	Killed	NKG
Sgt	C	Wignall	1075891	RAF(VR)	AG	Killed	NKG
Sgt	R	Haslam	494074	RAF(VR)	AG	Killed	NKG

Presumed crashed into the sea.

25/26th February 1943			**Nuremburg**			**Lancaster ED526 PO-J**	
W/O	M P	Stewart	A405189	RAAF	P	Killed	Durnbach (Ger)
Sgt	R M	Wylie	982917	RAF(VR)	FE	Killed	Durnbach (Ger)
F/Lt	O G	Rowcroft	A401196	RAAF	Nav	Killed	Durnbach (Ger)
WO2	R S	Woolley	R77317	RCAF	Wop	Killed	Durnbach (Ger)
Sgt	E	O'Kane	1479311	RAF(VR)	Obs	Killed	Durnbach (Ger)
Sgt	R	Wiggins	1321793	RAF(VR)	AG	Killed	Durnbach (Ger)
F/Sgt	L B	Larin	R73774	RCAF	AG	Killed	Durnbach (Ger)

Aircraft shot down 12 miles NW of Nurnburg.

11/12th March 1943 — **Stuttgart** — **Lancaster ED523 PO-**

P/O	G S	Mant	A405131	RAAF	P	Killed	Durnbach (Ger)
W/O	J J	Rider	1157637	RAF(VR)	FE	POW	
F/Lt	J	Leitke	A403058	RAAF	Nav	POW	
F/Sgt	G H	Millett	A404884	RAAF	Wop	Killed	Durnbach (Ger)
F/Lt	V G T	Davis	104376	RAF(VR)	AB	POW	
W/O	A E	Spencer	628624	RAF(VR)	AG	POW	
W/O	G R	Castle	A420441	RAAF	AG	POW	

3/4th April 1943 — **Essen** — **Lancaster ED524 PO-T**

S/Ldr	A M	Paape DFC	36192	RAF	P	Killed	Reichswald (Ger)
Sgt	L T	Fulcher	R61529	RCAF	FE	Killed	Reichswald (Ger)
F/O	H	North	116791	RAF(VR)	Nav	Killed	Reichswald (Ger)
F/O	T	Dring	129462	RAF(VR)	Wop/AG	Killed	Reichswald (Ger)
Sgt	D J R	Robinson	778674	RAF(VR)	AB	Killed	Reichswald (Ger)
Sgt	W	Johnson	1220311	RAF(VR)	AG	Killed	Reichswald (Ger)
F/O	J M	Stewart	131808	RAF(VR)	AG	Killed	Reichswald (Ger)

Aircraft shot down near Dusseldorf.

8th April 1943

ACW2	P	Austin	2135303	WAAF	Died	Bramley (UK)

Died in diphtheria epidemic.

16/17th April 1943 — **Pilsen** — **Lancaster ED651 PO-Y**

P/O	B C	Wilson	A408545	RAAF	P	POW	
Sgt	R H	Pallender	640100	RAF	FE	Killed	Rheinberg (Ger)
F/Lt	R	Stitt	127982	RAF(VR)	Nav	POW	
Sgt	H F	Goode	1382764	RAF(VR)	Wop/AG	Killed	Rheinberg (Ger)
P/O	F J	Boswell	127118	RAF(VR)	AB	POW	
Sgt	R	Dunn	944720	RAF(VR)	AG	Killed	Rheinberg (Ger)
Sgt	W W	Bannatyne	1564310	RAF(VR)	AG	Killed	Rheinberg (Ger)

16/17th April 1943 — **Pilsen** — **Lancaster ED771 PO-E**

F/Sgt	R C	Stewart	A406702	RAAF	P	Killed	Poix-de-la-Somme (Fr)
Sgt	T	Martin	636646	RAF	FE	Killed	Poix-de-la-Somme (Fr)
F/O	B R	McNair DFC	80418	RAF(VR)	Nav	Killed	Poix-de-la-Somme (Fr)
Sgt	R C	Anderson	A415980	RAAF	Wop/AG	Killed	Poix-de-la-Somme (Fr)
Sgt	A F	McDonald	1338233	RAF(VR)	Obs	Killed	Poix-de-la-Somme (Fr)
Sgt	P L	Boase	A405819	RAAF	AG	Killed	Poix-de-la-Somme (Fr)
Sgt	R J	Johnson	1453416	RAF(VR)	AG	Killed	Poix-de-la-Somme (Fr)

30th April/1st May 1943 — **Essen** — **Lancaster ED745 PO-**

F/Lt	R A	Craigie	40210	RAF(VR)	P	POW	
Sgt	W T	Fair	929876	RAF(VR)	FE	POW	
F/O	R H	Capron	127066	RAF(VR)	Nav	Killed	Harderwijk (NL)
F/O	G J	Phillips	130512	RAF(VR)	AB	POW	
Sgt	G H	Edwards	1078045	RAF(VR)	Wop	Killed	Harderwijk (NL)
Sgt	T D	Peat	1559144	RAF(VR)	AG	Killed	Harderwijk (NL)
Sgt	J A	Proctor	1520443	RAF(VR)	AG	Killed	Harderwijk (NL)

13/14th May 1943			Pilsen			Lancaster ED543 PO-H	
P/O	K E	Mahoney	A416223	RAAF	P	Killed	Hanover (Ger)
Sgt	B G	Hickling	1185786	RAF(VR)	FE	Killed	Hanover (Ger)
F/O	E F H	Heard	128665	RAF(VR)	Nav	Killed	Hanover (Ger)
Sgt	W G	Berry	1368760	RAF(VR)	AB	Killed	Hanover (Ger)
Sgt	M B	Squires	138828	RAF(VR)	Wop	Killed	Hanover (Ger)
Sgt	H W	Cox	1586740	RAF(VR)	AG	Killed	Hanover (Ger)
F/Sgt	B L	Haley	R131435	RCAF	AG	Killed	Hanover (Ger)

25/26th May 1943			Dusseldorf			Lancaster ED695 PO-J	
F/O	R S	Giddey	A6157	RAAF	P	POW	
Sgt	S G	Kiers	A9430	RAAF	FE	POW	
P/O	P R	Collins	133467	RAF(VR)	Nav	POW	
F/Sgt	W V	Morris	1337061	RAF(VR)	AB	POW	
Sgt	R J	Avann	1335033	RAF(VR)	Wop	POW	
F/Sgt	A F	Birkbeck	R102142	RCAF	AG	Killed	Flushing (NL)
P/O	K R	Langhorne	134377	RAF(VR)	AG	Killed	Flushing (NL)

25/26th May 1943			Dusseldorf			Lancaster ED768 PO-N	
F/Sgt	J M	Parsons	A409274	RAAF	P	Killed	Schoonselhof (NL)
Sgt	B	Spencer	574332	RAF	FE	Killed	Schoonselhof (NL)
Sgt	P J	Egan	1380187	RAF(VR)	Nav	POW	
Sgt	N J	Vaulkhard	1099743	RAF(VR)	AB	POW	
Sgt	J F	Selman	R92596	RCAF	Wop	POW	
Sgt	R A	Hunt	1609818	RAF(VR)	AG	POW	
Sgt	T	Chalmers	1401894	RAF(VR)	AG	Killed	Schoonselhof (NL)

Shot down by flak and crashed at Gravenwegel, Netherlands.

27/28th May 1943			Essen			Lancaster ED504 PO-K	
F/Lt	J M	Desmond	A406641	RAAF	P	Killed	Reichswald(Ger)
Sgt	E S	Davis	575812	RAF	FE	Killed	Reichswald(Ger)
P/O	G	Cribben	143426	RAF(VR)	Nav	Killed	Reichswald(Ger)
W/O	G F	Padden	650462	RAF(VR)	Wop	Killed	Reichswald(Ger)
P/O	J N	Lockwood	143430	RAF(VR)	AB	Killed	Reichswald(Ger)
F/O	C K	Cazaly	132388	RAF(VR)	AG	Killed	Reichswald(Ger)
P/O	J R	Ryalls	A405217	RAAF	AG	Killed	Reichswald(Ger)

Damaged in combat with a nightfighter. Crashed at Hartmann, 3 km NE of Barlo, Germany. Exploded on impact creating a crater 50 yards across. German fighter crashed on return to its base.

11/12th June 1943			Dusseldorf			Lancaster ED304 PO-C	
F/Sgt	B F	Wilmot	A401083	RAAF	P	Killed	NKG
Sgt	A	MacDonald	980916	RAF(VR)	FE	Killed	NKG
F/Sgt	T W	Hill	1388792	RAF(VR)	Nav	Killed	NKG
Sgt	W N	Cross	A412114	RAAF	Wop	Killed	NKG
Sgt	K T	White	1390403	RAF(VR)	AB	Killed	NKG
Sgt	W J	Fraser	1345138	RAF(VR)	AG	Killed	NKG
Sgt	W	Calvert	1349352	RAF(VR)	AG	Killed	NKG

Presumed crashed into the sea.

11/12th June 1943			Dusseldorf			Lancaster W4983 PO-B	
S/Ldr	D C	MacKenzie DFC	43706	RAF	P	Killed	Reichswald (Ger)
Sgt	J F	McLuskey	990173	RAF(VR)	FE	Killed	Reichswald (Ger)
P/O	D C	Bovis	145177	RAF(VR)	Nav	Killed	Reichswald (Ger)
F/O	L	Pietsch	A408779	RAAF	Wop	Killed	Reichswald (Ger)
Sgt	A D	Moore	657599	RAF(VR)	AB	Killed	Reichswald (Ger)
F/Lt	L R	Betts	115097	RAF(VR)	AG	Killed	Reichswald (Ger)
F/Sgt	J B	Donohue	A420614	RAAF	AG	Killed	Reichswald (Ger)
S/Ldr	B S	Ambrose	40040	RAF(VR)	2nd P	Killed	Reichswald (Ger)

16/17th June 1943 **Cologne** **Lancaster ED737 PO-F**

F/Sgt	J E	Binnie DFM	A414290	RAAF	P	POW	
Sgt	N M	Turnbull	649185	RAF	FE	Killed	Reichswald (Ger)
Sgt	R L	Godden	658613	RAF(VR)	Nav	Killed	Reichswald (Ger)
F/O	G H	Joseph	A400415	RAAF	Wop	Killed	Reichswald (Ger)
Sgt	K M	Taylor	1237051	RAF(VR)	AB	Killed	Reichswald (Ger)
Sgt	E V	Dean	R137269	RCAF	AG	POW	
Sgt	J M	Lancake	69116	RAF(VR)	AG	POW	
F/O	A	Smith	120058	RAF(VR)	2nd P	POW	

Aircraft shot down by a nightfighter. Sgt Taylor killed in the first pass.

28/29th June 1943 **Cologne** **Lancaster ED363 PO-E**

F/Sgt	R I	Gates	A415132	RAAF	P	Killed	NKG
Sgt	G R S	Cayless	1456974	RAF(VR)	FE	Killed	Jonkerbos (NL)
Sgt	H H	Mooney	655855	RAF	Nav	Killed	Jonkerbos (NL)
W/O	B H	Dolby	1313545	RAF(VR)	Wop	POW	
W/O	H G	Pike	1345238	RAF(VR)	AB	POW	
W/O2	T W J	Copeland	R129552	RCAF	AG	Killed	Jonkerbos (NL)
Sgt	J G	Hole	1337529	RAF(VR)	AG	Killed	Jonkerbos (NL)

Shot down by nightfighter, crashed at St Oldilienburg, Netherlands.

12/13th July 1943 **Turin** **Lancaster ED531 PO-T**

F/O	G D	Mitchell	A416693	RAAF	P	Killed	Vevy (Switz)
Sgt	B K H	Evans	1031846	RAF(VR)	FE	Killed	Vevy (Switz)
F/O	H R	St George	A414737	RAAF	Nav	Killed	Vevy (Switz)
F/Sgt	J M	Maher	A409844	RAAF	Wop	Killed	Vevy (Switz)
F/O	W H	Morgan	134667	RAF(VR)	AB	Killed	Vevy (Switz)
F/Sgt	H B	Bolger	A414193	RAAF	AG	Killed	Vevy (Switz)
F/Sgt	A D	Terry	A19117	RAAF	AG	Killed	Vevy (Switz)

Collided with high tension cables above Thyon in the Swiss Alps following partial jettisoning of bomb load. Crashed and burnt out, 0120 hrs (Swiss time).

12/13th July 1943 **Turin** **Lancaster JA676 PO-B**

F/Lt	R W A	Gibbs	40468	RAF	P	Killed	NKG
Sgt	E A	Roper	1623211	RAF(VR)	FE	Killed	NKG
F/O	S G	Norris	132148	RAF(VR)	Nav	Killed	NKG
Sgt	D J	Banks	1153128	RAF(VR)	Wop	Killed	NKG
F/O	J E	Pearce	130290	RAF(VR)	AB	Killed	NKG
P/O	S O'C	Tate	138889	RAF(VR)	AG	Killed	NKG
Sgt	D A	Chisholm	1052247	RAF(VR)	AG	Killed	NKG

Probably crashed in the Bay of Biscay on the return flight.

12/13th July 1943 **Turin** **Lancaster LM311 PO-L**

P/O	C A	Chapman	A415117	RAAF	P	Killed	Oxford (UK)
Sgt	J	Greenwood	980381	RAF(VR)	FE	Killed	Todmorden (UK)
Sgt	A E	Michaels	1551320	RAF(VR)	Nav	Killed	Glasgow (UK)
Sgt	P	Donlevy	1369188	RAF(VR)	Wop	Killed	Dalkeith (UK)
Sgt	N C	Smith	1349535	RAF(VR)	AB	Killed	Edinburgh (UK)
F/Sgt	W	Bruce	967187	RAF(VR)	AG	Killed	Falkirk (UK)
Sgt	W S	Buchanan	1372826	RAF(VR)	AG	Killed	Glasgow (UK)

Broke up on final approach due to flak damage. Crashed and burnt out.

16/17th July 1943 **Cislago** **Lancaster EE194 PO-E**

Sgt	A E	Murray	1320579	RAF(VR)	Nav	Killed	El Alia (Algiers)

Killed in fighter attack over target.

27/28th July 1943 | **Hamburg** | **Lancaster W4946 PO-Ū**

F/Sgt	J T	Buchanan	A405998	RAAF	P	Killed	Terschelling (NL)
Sgt	G C	Peggs	1615594	RAF(VR)	FE	Killed	NKG
P/O	A L	Gibbons	A415245	RAAF	Nav	Killed	Terschelling (NL)
P/O	K H	Hoffman	A414798	RAAF	Wop	Killed	Terschelling (NL)
F/Sgt	R P	Holmes	A414351	RAAF	AB	Killed	Terschelling (NL)
F/Sgt	D E S	Dean	A408307	RAAF	AG	Killed	Terschelling (NL)
F/Sgt	R G	Reu	A417416	RAAF	AG	Killed	Terschelling (NL)

Shot down by Hauptmann Jabs of IV/NJG1.

27/28th July 1943 | **Hamburg** | **Lancaster W5003 PO-H**

P/O	J L	Carrington	A413167	RAAF	P	Killed	Hamburg (Ger)
Sgt	E C	Brookes	482399	RAF(VR)	FE	POW	
F/Sgt	M R W	King	1315580	RAF(VR)	Nav	Killed	Hamburg (Ger)
Sgt	W	Green	1081353	RAF(VR)	Wop	Killed	Hamburg (Ger)
Sgt	H V	Hawkins	658138	RAF(VR)	AB	Killed	Hamburg (Ger)
Sgt	H	Bradley	620508	RAF	AG	Killed	Hamburg (Ger)
Sgt	S	Drake		RAF(VR)	AG	POW	

Shot down by fighter.

29/30th July 1943 | **Hamburg** | **Lancaster ED534 PO-R**

F/Sgt	R W	Park	A414118	RAAF	P	Killed	NKG
Sgt	G	Hopkins	1415465	RAF(VR)	FE	Killed	NKG
F/Sgt	J R	Chapman	A414992	RAAF	Nav	Killed	NKG
F/Sgt	R C	McBean	A409478	RAAF	Wop	Killed	NKG
Sgt	M J	McMahon	A422243	RAAF	AB	Killed	NKG
Sgt	H O	Hillier	A420566	RAAF	AG	Killed	NKG
F/Sgt	D A	Reid	A414080	RAAF	AG	Killed	NKG

2/3rd August 1943 | **Hamburg** | **Lancaster JA906 PO-**

Sgt	B N	Pratt	1262759	RAF(VR)	AG	Killed	Long Bennington (UK)

Killed in fighter attack.

3 August 1943 | **Training** | **Lancaster EO500 PO-**

F/O	J W	Nancarrow	A408867	RAAF	P	Injured
Sgt	T F	Preston	965739	RAFVR	E	Safe
F/O	M C	Fry	130598	RAFVR	N	Safe
Sgt	W S	Millar	1487423	RAFVR	Wop	Safe
Sgt	W	Cullen	1515885	RAFVR	AB	Safe
Sgt	G C	Borradale	1332645	RAFVR	AG	Safe

Four hours into a night training flight three engines failed. The crew baled out with the exception of F/O Nancarrow who crash-landed the aircraft at 1230 hours at Park Farm, 3 miles S of Audlem, Cheshire.

15/16th August 1943 | **Milan** | **Lancaster ED998 PO-Y**

W/Cdr	C L	Gomm DSO DFC	34123	RAF	P	Killed	St. Désir (Fr)
Sgt	J R	Lee	575842	RAF(VR)	FE	POW	
F/O	K	Gibson	137520	RAF(VR)	Nav	Killed	St. Désir (Fr)
F/O	A H	Reardon	A411520	RAAF	Wop	Killed	St. Désir (Fr)
F/O	T J	Phillips	126448	RAF(VR)	AB	Killed	St. Désir (Fr)
P/O	H N	Pritchard	52099	RAF	AG	Killed	St. Désir (Fr)
W/O	L L	McKenny	A416270	RAAF	AG	Killed	St. Désir (Fr)

Attacked by nightfighter over France on the outward journey. Exploded in mid-air scattering wreckage over 2 square miles around Beaumont-et-Loire.

15/16th August 1943			**Milan**			**Lancaster JA675 PO-**	
F/Lt	J McD	Sullivan	A404909	RAAF	P	Killed	Poix-de-la-Somme (Fr)
Sgt	J A E	Newland	959476	RAF	FE	Killed	Poix-de-la-Somme (Fr)
W/O	R E	Grange	R54227	RCAF	Nav	POW	
Sgt	K L	Harvey	1211431	RAF(VR)	Wop	POW	
F/O	T H	Entract	134770	RAF(VR)	AB	POW	
Sgt	L	Spurr	985455	RAF(VR)	AG	Killed	Poix-de-la-Somme (Fr)
Sgt	A P	Power	1396149	RAF(VR)	AG	Killed	Poix-de-la-Somme (Fr)

Believed shot down on return leg of journey.

17/18th August 1943			**Peenemunde**			**Lancaster ED764 PO-N**	
P/O	F W	Dixon	A412923	RAAF	P	POW	
Sgt	L C	Hayward	1464967	RAF(VR)	FE	Killed	Berlin (Ger)
Sgt	E W	Dickson	1445095	RAF(VR)	Nav	POW	
W/O	P	Lowe	1218582	RAF(VR)	Wop	Killed	Berlin (Ger)
Sgt	C A	Bicknell	1388783	RAF(VR)	AB	POW	
Sgt	R	Hughes	1696212	RAF(VR)	AG	POW	
Sgt	R	Garnett	1451360	RAF(VR)	AG	POW	

Shot down by fighter in the target area, believed to have been that of Leutnant Peter Erhardt of II/NJG5. Crashed into the sea off Peenemunde.

17/18th August 1943			**Peenemunde**			**Lancaster LM342 PO-**	
S/Ldr	A S	Raphael	68155	RAF(VR)	P	Killed	NKG
Sgt	V	Smith	980905	RAF(VR)	FE	Killed	NKG
F/O	R G	Carter	J15862	RCAF	Nav	Killed	NKG
P/O	D	Fielden	149478	RAF(VR)	Wop	Killed	NKG
Sgt	F	Grey	1317456	RAF(VR)	AB	Killed	NKG
Sgt	A C	Brand	1353125	RAF(VR)	AG	Killed	Poznan (Pol)
F/Sgt	F B	Garrett	1154625	RAF(VR)	AG	Killed	NKG
F/Lt	M H	Parry	126019	RAF(VR)	2nd AB	Killed	NKG

Crashed into the Kölpien See next to the Peenemunde research station. Sgt Brand fell clear of the wreckage and was washed ashore in Poland.

23/24th August 1943			**Berlin**			**Lancaster JB124 PO-**	
F/Sgt	H R	Vincent	A416635	RAAF	P	Killed	NKG
Sgt	J M	Jones	650138	RAF	FE	Killed	NKG
F/Sgt	W G	Hurle	A409411	RAAF	Nav	Killed	NKG
F/Sgt	L C	Fitzner	A414667	RAAF	Wop	Killed	NKG
Sgt	F G	McIntyre	A420703	RAAF	AB	Killed	NKG
F/Sgt	R F	Holdaway	1259359	RAF(VR)	AG	Killed	NKG
F/Sgt	D P R	Schubert	A414602	RAAF	AG	Killed	NKG

Presumed crashed into the sea.

27/28th August 1943			**Nuremburg**			**Lancaster EE194 PO-E**	
F/O	M R	Good	A285324	RAAF	P	Killed	Durnbach (Ger)
Sgt	J A	Beck	641951	RAF	FE	Killed	Durnbach (Ger)
F/Sgt	B	Kerlin	A413610	RAAF	Nav	Killed	Durnbach (Ger)
F/Sgt	A F	Loxton	A414710	RAAF	Wop	Killed	Durnbach (Ger)
F/Sgt	R H	Hallam	A414348	RAAF	AB	Killed	Durnbach (Ger)
Sgt	W E	Hogarth	R149420	RCAF	AG	Killed	Durnbach (Ger)
F/Sgt	A F	Dodson	A417348	RAAF	AG	Killed	Durnbach (Ger)

3/4th September 1943			Berlin			Lancaster DV237 PO-	
P/O	R V	Turner	149548	RAF(VR)	P	Killed	Berlin (Ger)
Sgt	J A	Stewart	636350	RAF	FE	Killed	NKG
F/Sgt	I D	Jennings	R130022	RCAF	Nav	Killed	Berlin (Ger)
Sgt	D B	Richardson	1123968	RAF(VR)	Wop	Killed	Berlin (Ger)
Sgt	E	Robson	1553859	RAF	FE	Killed	NKG
Sgt	L A	Price	1580639	RAF(VR)	AG	Killed	Berlin (Ger)
Sgt	W C	McCartney	1370097	RAF(VR)	AG	Killed	NKG

3/4th September 1943			Berlin			Lancaster ED541 PO-A	
F/Lt	R	Carmichael	A412391	RAAF	P	Killed	NKG
Sgt	L A	Saunders	A14472	RAAF	FE	Killed	NKG
F/O	P E	Henley	128547	RAF(VR)	Nav	Killed	NKG
Sgt	R T J	Bilney	129024	RAF(VR)	Wop	Killed	Berlin (Ger)
Sgt	N E	Burgess	1274974	RAF(VR)	AB	Killed	Berlin (Ger)
Sgt	O H	Hodges	1301508	RAF(VR)	AG	Killed	Berlin (Ger)
F/Sgt	C H	Niven	R147502	RCAF	AG	Killed	NKG
F/Sgt	R	Lesser	R117456	RCAF	2nd AB	Killed	Berlin (Ger)

23/24th September 1943			Mannheim			Lancaster DV233 PO-	
P/O	W T	Farmer	A416843	RAAF	P	Killed	NKG
Sgt	R V	Chinnery	1642934	RAF(VR)	FE	POW	
P/O	A	Puttick	134545	RAF(VR)	Nav	POW	
Sgt	T W	Darvill	1331414	RAF(VR)	Wop	POW	
Sgt	J	Knowles	1138898	RAF(VR)	AB	POW	
Sgt	P	Cansfield	1130730	RAF(VR)	AG	POW	
F/Sgt	C E	Adair	A11615	RAAF	AG	Killed	Durnbach (Ger)

23/24th September 1943			Mannheim			Lancaster EE135 PO-Y	
P/O	A	Long	A413396	RAAF	P	Killed	Durnbach (Ger)
Sgt	C	Weddell	1603571	RAF(VR)	FE	Killed	Durnbach (Ger)
F/Sgt	O J	Lumsden	A413779	RAAF	Nav	Killed	Durnbach (Ger)
Sgt	J B	Harrison	1485062	RAF(VR)	Wop	Killed	Durnbach (Ger)
W/O 2	M C	Craik	R110957	RCAF	AB	Killed	Durnbach (Ger)
F/Sgt	H A	Green	R147218	RCAF	AG	Killed	Durnbach (Ger)
Sgt	T T B	Francis	1424559	RAF(VR)	AG	Killed	Durnbach (Ger)

2/3rd October 1943			Munich			Lancaster ED530 PO-O	
P/O	K A	McIver DFC	A412036	RAAF	P	Killed	North Walsham (UK)
F/Sgt	J K	Gale	1490465	RAF(VR)	Nav	Killed	NKG
Sgt	C	MacLean	1330142	RAF(VR)	Wop	Killed	NKG
F/Sgt	M E	McGrath	1389498	RAF(VR)	AB	Safe	
Sgt	A B	McLelland	6206056	RAF	FE	Killed	Bergen op Zoom (NL)
Sgt	R	Short	639991	RAF	AG	Killed	NKG
F/Sgt	F W	Shaw	1321440	RAF(VR)	AG	Killed	NKG

Ditched in the sea 0150 hrs 25 miles off Beachy Head due to lack of fuel. F/Sgt McGrath picked up in dinghy on following day, the sole survivor.

2/3rd October 1943 | **Munich** | **Lancaster ED621 PO-P**

P/O	R	Harder	NZ415692	RNZAF	P	Killed	Durnbach (Ger)
Sgt	G K	Barnes	546801	RAF(VR)	FE	Killed	Durnbach (Ger)
F/Sgt	G E	Potter	A410088	RAAF	Nav	Killed	Durnbach (Ger)
Sgt	W J	Baker	1334345	RAF(VR)	Wop	Killed	NKG
F/O	M E	Garbutt	A413976	RAAF	AB	Killed	Durnbach (Ger)
Sgt	N	Sidaway	1499834	RAF(VR)	AG	Killed	Durnbach (Ger)
F/Sgt	F	Pullom	A414161	RAAF	AG	Killed	Durnbach (Ger)
F/Sgt	A W	Wright	A418609	RAAF	2nd Nav	Killed	Durnbach (Ger)

3/4th October 1943 | **Kassel** | **Lancaster JA906 PO-**

P/O	G J	Smith	A414385	RAAF	P	POW	
Sgt	A	Proudfoot	1551970	RAF(VR)	FE	POW	
F/Sgt	R E	Dallwitz	A409669	RAAF	Nav	Killed	Flushing (NL)
F/Sgt	R E	Brook	A414460	RAAF	Wop	Killed	NKG
F/Sgt	J E	Francis	A409579	RAAF	AB	Killed	NKG
F/Sgt	S E	Jackson	A416679	RAAF	AG	Killed	Flushing (NL)
F/Sgt	R G	Wellington	A421483	RAAF	AG	POW	

8/9th October 1943 | **Hanover** | **Lancaster JA902 PO-**

F/Sgt	J W	O'Connor	A420990	RAAF	Wop	POW

Collided with fighter over target causing extensive damage.

18/19th October 1943 | **Hanover** | **Lancaster W4240 PO-**

F/O	F S	Davenport	A18071	RAAF	P	Killed	Hanover (Ger)
Sgt	F G	Newton	1801399	RAF(VR)	FE	Killed	Hanover (Ger)
F/O	S H	Hollerin	138468	RAF(VR)	Nav	POW	
Sgt	F G	Beardwell	1334654	RAF(VR)	Wop	Killed	Hanover (Ger)
F/O	J R	Fisher	132807	RAF(VR)	AB	Killed	Hanover (Ger)
Sgt	T J	Clark	1581159	RAF(VR)	AG	Killed	Hanover (Ger)
Sgt	J L	Killan	1351860	RAF(VR)	AG	Killed	Hanover (Ger)

22/23rd October 1943 | **Kassel** | **Lancaster DV226 PO-**

P/O	G P	Godwin DFC	A401845	RAAF	P	Killed	NKG
Sgt	W H	Thornhill	1464625	RAF(VR)	FE	Killed	NKG
P/O	J E	Cox	156916	RAF(VR)	Nav	Killed	NKG
Sgt	F H	Bloomfield	1331745	RAF(VR)	Wop	Killed	NKG
F/Sgt	H	Telford	1099681	RAF(VR)	AB	Killed	NKG
Sgt	G	Blake-Hales	1267121	RAF(VR)	AG	Killed	NKG
F/Sgt	A	King	1316916	RAF(VR)	AG	Killed	NKG

Presumed crashed into the sea.

3/4th November 1943 | **Dusseldorf** | **Lancaster JB121 PO-U**

S/Ldr	W J	Lewis DFC	63071	RAF	P	Killed	Schoonselhof (Bel)
Sgt	C E	Stead	941072	RAF(VR)	FE	POW	
F/Sgt	K	Garvey	1075988	RAF(VR)	Nav	Evaded	
Sgt	R C	Morley	1230169	RAF(VR)	Wop	Evaded	
P/O	A J	Scott	159896	RAF(VR)	AB	Killed	Schoonselhof (Bel)
Sgt	G P	Baylis	613449	RAF	AG	Killed	Schoonselhof (Bel)
P/O	J W	Evans	A410152	RAAF	2nd Nav	POW	

Aircraft suffered flak hit in the bomb bay causing a fire. Captain gave order to bale out, aircraft crashing in Belgium.

1668 HEAVY CONVERSION UNIT ROYAL AIR FORCE

12 December 1944 **Training** **Lancaster JA908**

F/O	L	Richer	41162	RAFVR	P	Safe	

Crash landed on three engines on second attempt, aircraft caught fire and was destroyed.

15th January 1945 **Training** **Lancaster LM619**

F/O	I V L	Thompson	A429081	RAAF	P	Killed	Oxford (UK)
Sgt	J	Rawlinson	2218660	RAF(VR)	FE	Killed	Bootle (UK)
Sgt	J G	Hazelden	1623968	RAF(VR)	Nav	Killed	Rainford (UK)
F/Sgt	A B	Thomas	A429069	RAAF	Wop	Killed	Oxford (UK)
Sgt	C R	Mann	1586368	RAF(VR)	AB	Killed	Cheltenham (UK)
Sgt	D G	Burn	1251125	RAF(VR)	AG	Killed	Tottenham (UK)
Sgt	G F	Ashby	1629627	RAF(VR)	AG	Injured	

Crashed at Westborough, Lincs., 2030 hrs whilst engaged in a light bombing exercise.

7 February 1945 **Training** **Lancaster JA684**

F/O		Walker	196914	RAFVR	Instructor	Safe
F/O	F G	Wilkinson	J35380	RCAF	Pupil	Safe

Hit strawstacks after touching down beyond threshold whilst practising three engine overshoots - burnt out. Three crewmembers injured.

10 March 1945 **Training** **Lancaster JB338**

F/Sgt	J P	Paddison		RAFVR	P	Safe

Crashed at Fiskerton after port outer engine had been feathered and the aircraft had got partially out of control. Aircraft burnt out.